A FAR-FLUNG GAMBLE

Havana 1762

DAVID GREENTREE

First published in Great Britain in 2010 by Osprey Publishing,
Midland House, West Way, Botley, Oxford, OX2 0PH, UK
44–02 23rd St, Suite 219, Long Island City, NY 11101, USA
E-mail: info@ospreypublishing.com

© 2010 Osprey Publishing Ltd.

Print ISBN: 978 1 84603 987 4
PDF e-book ISBN: 978 1 84603 988 1

Page layout by: Bounford.com, Cambridge, UK
Index by Michael Forder
Typeset in Sabon
Maps by Bounford.com, Cambridge, UK
Originated by United Graphics, Singapore
Printed in China through Worldprint

10 11 12 13 14   10 9 8 7 6 5 4 3 2 1

A CIP catalogue record for this book is available from the British Library.

THE WOODLAND TRUST

Osprey Publishing are supporting the Woodland Trust, the UK's leading
woodland conservation charity, by funding the dedication of trees.

ACKNOWLEDGEMENTS

I would like to thank Adrian Jones for his photos of Havana,
David Campbell for reading the script and making many worthwhile
suggestions, Alison Williams for visiting the *Museo Naval* in Madrid,
Flori Libreros for translating Spanish sources and helping me with my
communications with the *Museo Naval*, Jenny Wraight at the Naval
Historical Branch in Portsmouth, Geoff Banks for his photos of the
Admiralty Library collection, the University of Buffalo for generously
supplying me with a copy of Roswell Park's Journal, Dr Gustavo Placer
Cervera, and Philip MacKie of the Seven Year's War Association. My thanks
are also due to the Portsmouth Central Library, the British Library, the
Royal Marines Museum, the National Maritime Museum, Bridgeman Arts,
and Peter Harrington at the Anne SK Brown Collection. This book is
dedicated to my father.

CONTENTS

INTRODUCTION

In the early afternoon of 30 July 1762, three officers, each leading 12 men, prepared to storm El Morro fortress. The first group was commanded by Lieutenant Forbes of the Royal Scots, the second by Lieutenant Holyrod of the 90th Foot, and the third by Lieutenant Nugent of the 9th Foot. All were probably veterans of previous amphibious operations, but only one would survive the day.

El Morro dominated the entrance to Havana Harbour, and its capture was seen as integral to a successful outcome of a siege of the town. Its commander, Captain Velasco, had refused to be bombarded into submission and so forced the British to launch an assault. The attack would be the decisive moment of an expedition the government had ordered in January, the culmination of the last and perhaps most ambitious British operation of the Seven Years War.

By 1762, Britain had been at war for six years against a coalition of countries led by France and which included Austria and Russia. Prussia, their only ally on the continent, had fended off the coalition's armies but was reaching breaking point. Britain was also straining its military and financial sinews, firstly by fighting the French in far-flung corners of the globe, and

In 1589 Philip II ordered the construction of two castles either side of the narrow entrance to the harbour. The smaller, La Punta, can be seen here from the larger, more imposing fort called El Morro. By the middle of the 18th century Havana, with a population of 35,000, was the largest city in the Caribbean.

secondly by subsidizing both the Prussian Army and a combined British and German force on the European continent. In late 1761, when the finances of both sides had reached near-exhaustion and peace seemed on the horizon, intelligence suggested that Spain was preparing to join the coalition; now there would be no end in sight unless Britain could, through a timely pre-emptive strike, knock Spain out with a decisive blow. The main effort would be against Havana, the fabled key to the Caribbean; in the Pacific an expedition to Manila in the Philippines would be a smaller but equally ambitious enterprise.

These operations recalled the days of privateer raiding by Drake in the 16th and Morgan in the 17th centuries, but now as colonial defences became more formidable, so too did the attacks brought to bear against them. The force sent to capture Havana needed to be of a size that only a state machine could muster; in all, the expedition would comprise units already in the Caribbean trying to seize the French island of Martinique, units specifically dispatched from Britain, and others to be transported from New York (including North American provincial regiments). This concentration of manpower was necessary because yellow fever could destroy armies in the Caribbean – in the 1741 campaign to capture Cartagena (in present-day Colombia), out of approximately 10,000 soldiers that actually landed, only 3,549 were listed as fit when the force re-embarked. Furthermore, unlike earlier raids, the aim at Havana was not to attack, plunder, and leave, but to seize and hold a valuable bargaining asset, and for this a larger force was required.

Founded in 1514, Havana's natural harbour was one of the largest in the world and could accommodate up to 1,000 sail. This and the position of the

By 1634 a Spanish royal decree declared Havana the 'Key of the new World and Bulwark of the West Indies'. However, by the 18th century Havana was not only a conduit for trade but also a valuable producer in its own right. (Bridgeman Art)

1514

Havana founded

prevailing Atlantic trade winds made the port the ideal rendezvous for Spanish galleons carrying gold and silver from the Spanish viceroyalties of Mexico and Peru to Cadíz in Spain. The town soon attracted the attention of privateers, was sacked and burned by pirates in 1537, plundered by the French in 1555, and threatened by Sir Francis Drake in 1586. The Spanish Government was convinced of the need for strong defences, and the town was one of the few in the Caribbean that was sited entirely within the confines of its own walls.

In 1761 Charles III of Spain wanted the assurance of a strong defence before involving the country in war. He believed 'if Havana is not secure, the American colonies will fall of their own weight'. He confided to his most trusted minister, Bernado Tanucci, that Spain could be joining the war, and arrangements needed to be made for such an eventuality. He had a personal animosity towards England, whom he described as having 'a universal despotism over the oceans', and feared that British success against France was adversely and irreversibly upsetting the balance of power. Despite the fortifications at the harbour entrance, Charles III identified that building defences on the heights east of the town, called La Cabaña, was 'the most important task in all of Spain's domains'. On 7 February 1761 a new governor arrived, Captain General Don Juan de Prado, accompanied by the French engineers, brothers Francisco and Baltasar Ricaud, to improve defences.

El Morro had 64 guns and a 700-man garrison but was overlooked by the heights of La Cabaña, which is the perspective shown here. La Cabaña had been identified in 1589 as integral to controlling the town, and in 1740 the *Gentleman's Magazine* wrote if these hills were occupied the town would not hold out for long.

In London, different interpretations of Spanish intentions were causing a government crisis. Pitt wanted a pre-emptive attack, but he was outvoted in cabinet and resigned from office in October 1761. However, the Spanish threat would not go away and Newcastle, the Prime Minister, had to make a decision regarding its mitigation. An attack on Havana had been considered during the War of Austrian Succession, and in 1754 Admiral Knowles (who had commanded a ship of the line in the attempt on Cartagena) had visited the town and written a report on the Spanish defences. All the evidence suggested Havana was the best place for Britain to strike, and the lesson from Cartagena was that operations had to be concluded before tropical disease took hold (commonly accepted to be six weeks after disembarkation) in order for disaster to be averted.

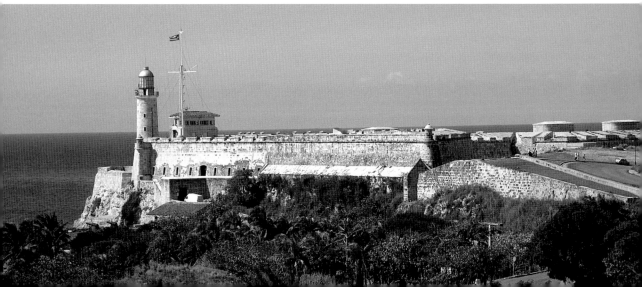

ORIGINS

Ever since the discovery of the New World, Spain's colonial possessions in the Caribbean had been ripe targets for plunder by other European powers, but France and Britain gradually assumed a more vested interest in the area as they developed settlements there. Sugar cane was grown on British Jamaica and the French islands of Martinique and Guadeloupe. As well as being valuable markets for manufactured goods produced in the mother country, colonies were now becoming producers of raw materials to supply the mother country. By 1759, Martinique produced 20,000 tons of sugar a year and traded with North America by undercutting Jamaican prices.

In the 1660s and 1670s, Charles II could use buccaneers like Morgan, who were eager for Spanish plunder, to successfully establish Jamaica as a permanent English colony; however, the first attempts between 1689 and 1692 to send expeditions of regular troops from Britain ended in failure. In the meantime, the French were improving their strategic position by acquiring half of Hispaniola from the Spanish in the 1690s. Ships based here could dominate the Windward Passage into the Caribbean and intercept British vessels sailing to Barbados and Antigua. French privateers from Martinique and Guadeloupe preyed on British commerce in the Caribbean, and, in the War of Austrian Succession (1740–48) over 1,000 British ships were seized. British warships stationed at Jamaica, far to leeward, could not effectively protect British trade. The expansion of British power in the region was at risk.

In the 18th century, the New World offered a myriad of different trading opportunities for European powers, but Spain, believing that a fixed amount of wealth existed in the world, jealously guarded this wealth by banning trade between its colonies and other countries. A Board of Trade was established to rigidly regulate and control commercial activity, and a convoy system called the *Flota a Neuve España* was developed to protect its conveyance, guarded by a permanent naval presence at Havana called the *Armada de Barlovento*. Spanish policy centred on severing economic links between Cuba and Jamaica, and forcing Cuba to trade with Spain.

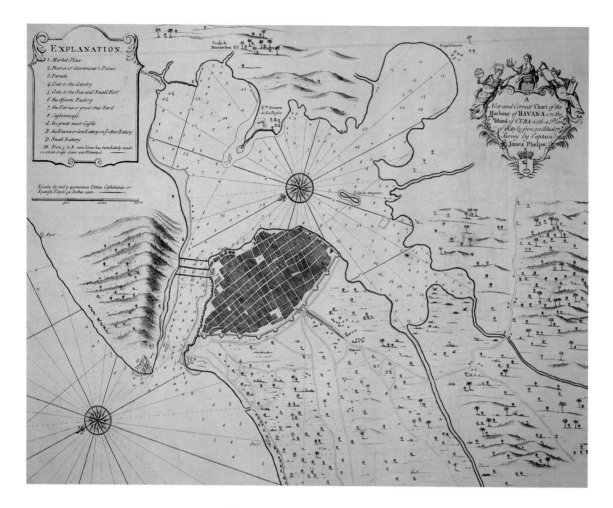

EXPLANATION.
1 Market Place
2 Fueroa or Governour's Palace
3 Parade
4 Gate to the Country
5 Gate to the Sea and Small Fort
6 the Agents Factory
7 the Fabrick or great ships Yard
8 Customhouse
a. the great moor Castle
B. the Fueroa or low Battery or of other Battery
D. Small Battery
N.B. From 3 to B new Lines has been Lately made on which Great Guns are Mounted

A New and Correct Chart of the Harbour of HAVANA on the Island of CUBA with a Plan of City &c from an Actual Survey by Captain James Phelps.

Britain became increasingly envious of this trade monopoly. In 1713, as part of the Treaty of Utrecht that ended the Spanish War of Succession, the British were permitted to send only a single 100-ton ship each year to trade with Latin America. By 1739, parliament wanted more and pushed Prime Minister Walpole into making war with Spain. A British squadron was now permanently stationed in the West Indies, and under Admiral Vernon it wrought havoc on Spanish trading outposts; however, the expedition sent from England to capture the fortified town of Cartagena in 1741 proved a costly failure, while a descent on Havana was considered too ambitious as its fortifications had an impregnable reputation.

At the mouth of the Gulf of Mexico, Havana was at a choke point along a vital sea route through which the Gulf Stream took the treasure ships to Spain; after the British seized Jamaica, ships transiting to Spain from Cartagena became vulnerable to attack, so the route via Havana had become more favoured. A treasure fleet in the Caribbean had never successfully been intercepted, though at times sailings were postponed. Spain would even risk a sea battle to defend the treasure fleet, a circumstance that occurred in 1748 when Admiral Reggio successfully fended off Knowles. In the War of Jenkins' Ear (1739–48), three fleets successfully made the voyage to Spain.

Regimiento de Voluntarios de Cavalleria de la Havana ᵟᵗᵉᵗᵒ.

Diseño del actual vestuario que usa este Cuerpo desde el año de 1765. de su creacion.

Nota.

Que usa de votines como se demuestra.

The costs of keeping regular troops in the colonies was three times more than those incurred in Spain and at any one time one-fifth would be sick; in contrast, the local militia were cheaper and were likely to have full immunity from yellow fever. As well as the presence of regular dragoon units from Spain, Havana also maintained a regiment of cavalry recruited locally. Illustrated here is a trooper from this unit. (Bridgeman Art)

Few European immigrants had settled in Havana because of the prevalence of yellow fever, a mosquito-borne virus imported from West Africa in 1648. (The virus can survive only above 16°C and the mosquito needs temperatures of above 27°C to flourish.) Between 1731 and 1762 there were six epidemics in Cuba. Because mosquitoes need stagnant water to prosper, and often favour containers with solid sides and flat bottoms like water casks, urban areas were particularly vulnerable. Adults were more susceptible than children, but nearly every adult in Havana had been infected as a child and those that survived had a lifelong immunity; European invaders would have no such benefit.

Despite the blight of tropical disease in its towns, with fertile soil and a climate capable of supporting the growth of the tobacco plant and sugar cane, Cuba benefited immensely from its hinterland – even if overproduction could lead to food shortages and a reliance on imports from Mexico during periods of drought. Mercantilist Spain enforced a state monopoly to buy tobacco leaf, which was managed from 1740 by local businessmen from the Havana Company; but, by seeking to control production, Spain was also limiting its growth and supply trailed behind demand. Enforcement of high quality controls to satisfy the state tobacco factories in Seville and efforts to combat contraband led to local resentment, and in 1720, to open revolt. Even so, from 1740 to 1760 tobacco generated 7–10 million peso per year (6–9 million peso being profit for the Crown, representing 25–33 per cent of total Spanish fiscal income). This was an amount more than enough to pay for either the costs of governing and defending Cuba or for running the entire Spanish Navy, and was equivalent to one-fifth of the value of the Peruvian silver mines. Revenue from sugar production paled in comparison, even though exports trebled between 1754 and 1760 (in part through contraband); the industry was similarly regulated by the state and had to compete for both labour and wood with the shipyard.

Of the 227 Spanish ships of the line built in the 18th century, about one-third ran down the slipways at Havana (from 1735 at the new shipyard known as Asterillo Real). Production costs were half of what they were in Spain because plentiful timber was close at hand and slaves could work in the yard. In comparison to ships made from European oak, ships made from Cuban cedar were more durable, capable of going twice as long before careening was necessary, and were safer as the wood was less likely to splinter when struck by cannon balls.

Havana was also a valuable base for privateers and the infamous Guarda Costa (coastguards), both of whom intercepted foreign vessels attempting to trade with Spanish colonies, and confiscated their cargoes. Merchant vessels, including the summer sugar fleets that sailed from Jamaica to North America through the channel between Cuba and Hispaniola, were intercepted from Havana and also from Santiago de Cuba, a port on the south coast of Cuba that could easily monitor British naval movements around Jamaica. From 1742 to 1745, some 99 British ships were seized sailing between Jamaica and New York, with Cuban privateers venturing as far as New York itself. In 1746, the British resorted to a direct blockade of Santiago de Cuba after an attempt to seize the port by amphibious assault had failed. From Havana, Spain also sought to secure and expand its North American continental possessions: supplies were regularly sent to Florida and in 1742, a 2,000-strong Spanish expedition departed to raid Georgia.

Despite Havana's utility as a naval base, the Spanish, with more extensive commitments to Imperial defence than Britain, were never able to use Havana to control the sea lanes. Defensive fortifications were always their priority and in 1725, spurred on by an unfavourable French report, 21 engineers were sent to the Caribbean, including four to Havana. With stores from Mexico, labour from the prisons and slaves, and funds from local import taxes and even local sponsorship, the defensive works were improved. Havana's 3-mile-long wall was defended from 1732 to 1762 by a garrison of 1,500–2,000 regulars, supplemented by a larger militia that in 1760 numbered 6,342 men. But, by assigning the city a predominantly economic rather than military role, in the event of hostilities Madrid risked making Havana less a thorn in the side of its competitors and more a ripe apple ready to be picked.

The outbreak of the Seven Years War did not lead to an immediate threat to the city, however. The war was prompted by colonial rivalry, but the dispute was between France and Britain over territory in North America, which escalated when the British and then the French decided to send regular army units from Europe. A belated, half-successful British effort to intercept the French provoked them into preparing for general war. At the same time a diplomatic revolution was under way in Europe. In 1755 Prussia, which had been an ally of France in the 1740s, approached Britain and the two countries signed a defensive agreement. Austria, Britain's ally in the 1740s, then signed a defensive alliance with France; the alliance was activated in 1756 when Frederick the Great of Prussia, aware of Austrian troop preparations to invade Silesia, made a pre-emptive attack. Ministers realized the importance that operations in the colonies would have on the outcome of the war in Europe. Referring to the Americas, Holdernesse, the Northern Secretary (the minister responsible for North America), wrote to Prime Minister Newcastle: 'Finally the bomb has burst … this event will make a speedy consideration of the measures to be taken here necessary.' Newcastle too wrote how 'good success there [North America] would now put us in a condition (I hope) to get well, and soon, out of this affair'. However, during the initial stages of the war, Spain (then ruled by Ferdinand VI) was determinedly neutral despite provocations by overzealous British privateers. Both economically and strategically, Havana would be an expensive loss.

INITIAL STRATEGY

Throughout the Seven Years War Britain acted defensively in Europe, aiding Frederick in the defence of Germany by a variety of means: providing him with a large financial subsidy, paying for northern German allies to sustain their armies in the field, committing increasing numbers of British troops to aid these German units, and by launching raids on the French coast to divert French army units from Germany. The campaign in America, on the other hand, offered a chance to win the war through offensive action. Between 1758 and 1760, Louisbourg, Quebec, and Montreal were taken and the French thrown out of Canada, creating a financial crisis in Paris that limited the support France could give its Austrian ally. Concurrently, Pitt sought to pursue an aggressive strategy in the Caribbean. He thought Guadeloupe alone was worth more than the whole of Canada because of its sugar cane. On 12 November 1758, under the command of General Hopson (an old favourite of George II), a total of 9,000 soldiers in 64 transports left Portsmouth for Martinique, escorted by ten ships of the line. Before the dispatch of this expedition, only two ships of the line and 2,000 men were stationed in the Caribbean.

The Caribbean expedition 1759

The course of this expedition showed how precarious amphibious operations could be. On 3 January 1759 the fleet reached Barbados, but had to wait ten days before stragglers (notably the hospital ship) caught up, so all hope of surprise was lost. The men were beginning to suffer from yellow fever, only 6,000 being fit for duty by the time a landing on Martinique was made. Such was the difficult nature of the terrain, Hopson found that despite facing only a small militia he simply did not have enough men to drag his 30 guns into position to breach the walls of Fort Royal, especially when a 5-mile diversion became necessary to bypass a steep ravine – a problem further compounded by the lack of nearby fresh water. He concluded the fort was unassailable, although only 5 miles from the landing beaches, and ordered re-embarkation.

**JANUARY 4
1762**

**Britain declares
war on Spain**

Hopson decided to redeploy to nearby Guadeloupe but died from the fever. His replacement Barrington implemented a change in approach. By threatening many landings and carrying out few, the 3,000 French militia on the island became disheartened and were thrown off balance. A successful British descent on Fort Louis split the island in two; an attempt to retake this fort by the French was hampered by further landings in their rear. One final landing took the town of Basse-Terre, and on 1 May the island's governor surrendered. In contrast to the attempt on Martinique, the assault on Guadeloupe seemed a winning template for combined operations in the Caribbean. The next day, however, the arrival of a French squadron of eight ships of the line from Brest with 600 Swiss troops and 2,000 French 'buccaneers' showed how precarious amphibious operations could be. Luckily the French Governor did not rescind his capitulation and the relieving force re-embarked. At this juncture, with only 1,500 men fit for duty, Barrington would surely have been overcome.

Relations with the Spanish

On 10 August 1759, Charles III, the King of Naples and Ferdinand's half-brother, became King of Spain. Ever since 1700 when Philippe of Anjou, the grandson of Louis XIV, had become King Felipe V of Spain, the French and Spanish monarchies had a close affinity. On 15 August 1761 Charles signed a secret Bourbon Family Compact with France stipulating that Spain would join France in early 1762 and co-ordinate offensive military operations. Pitt suspected the countries were drawing together and wanted pre-emptive action against Spain. However George III, who in 1760 had succeeded his German-born father, wanted a detachment from the continent and a quick end to the war. Disliking Newcastle and Pitt, the king inaugurated a ministerial revolution, which led to his former tutor, the pacific Lord Bute, attaining increasing influence in government.

In contrast, the French minister Choiseul encouraged a more bellicose Spanish attitude. He thought the threat of Spanish intervention would obtain rapid British acceptance of his peace proposals, which included demands for fishing rights off Newfoundland; however, by diplomatic conventions of the day, Britain viewed these proposals as a preliminary, negotiable position and rejected them. Choiseul decided to pursue a military solution and sought to deliberately ruin further negotiations, but surprisingly Bute, who had replaced Holdernesse as Northern

Anson, the First Lord of the Admiralty, became the chief advocate and driving force behind the planning of the expedition. He had no fear of bold enterprises, having taken his squadron on a three-year circumnavigation of the globe in 1741, which took the Spanish Pacific treasure galleon. (Anne SK Brown collection)

Secretary, sent word Britain was prepared to concede Newfoundland fishing rights including a drying station. However, the Bourbon Family Compact had just been signed and for Choiseul the time for negotiation was over.

In September Britain found out about the compact when Spanish dispatches were intercepted. Pitt again recommended initiating war before the treasure fleet could reach Cadíz, but all other ministers save one disagreed. The military chiefs also warned against war with Spain, Admiral Anson saying that his Mediterranean fleet was inadequate and General Ligonier predicting the strength of the Spanish Army at 80,000 men. On 2 October a cabinet meeting advocated a diplomatic approach, and Pitt resigned three days later.

In a surprising volte-face, which suggested his previous position was a ploy to force Pitt's resignation, Bute then pressed for full disclosure of the compact. On 19 November an ultimatum was sent to Spain stating that if it did not disavow an intention to act with Britain's enemies, a state of war would exist between the two countries. In preparation for hostilities, the Mediterranean squadron was strengthened by seven ships of the line to make a total of 19, but such was the pressure on British national credit Bute warned Newcastle: 'If we have a war with Spain we must give up the German war; it is not possible to carry on both.'

Spain refused to explain the compact. The treasure fleet arrived and Spain adopted a tone of defiance, proclaiming the country would no longer suffer France 'to run the risk of receiving such rigid laws as were prescribed by an insulting victor'. On 10 December a Spanish order to seize all British shipping was issued. On 26 December the British cabinet agreed to send troops to Portugal (which Spain was planning to invade) and on 4 January 1762 officially declared war.

The strategic position

Foremost amongst British concerns was the threat presented by the Spanish Navy, especially if it was to act in concert with its French counterpart. Spanish naval capability had experienced a period of decline in the 17th century, but by 1760 its budget was up to 70 per cent of what was spent on the army (whereas in France the comparable figure was 12 per cent). Larger ships were being built, with the first Spanish three-decker launched in 1732. Spanish ships had larger hulls than British designs, which gave them greater stability. However there were many failings, notably an inability to find a sufficient number of trained crewmen. The problem was exacerbated by Spain's warm climate that meant many ports intermittently endured bouts of yellow fever. The navy had to compete with the requirements of commerce, and harsh discipline discouraged service. In 1759, although 59,000 sailors were on the seamen's register, only 26,000 were available for naval service. The sailors that did enlist were given few chances to develop their sailing skills because of the tendency to leave warships in port to save money; sending a ship of the line to sea was four times more expensive than keeping it alongside. The most telling deficiency was the time required to reload a 32-pdr gun; Spanish crews took 5 minutes whereas a British crew took 90 seconds. The overall role of the Spanish Navy was to defend commerce and transport troops rather than confront an enemy squadron in battle, and its commanders believed battle should be the exception rather than the rule as, in their opinion, losing ships in combat would make these tasks more difficult.

In comparison, Britain had more than double the number of sailors. In 1756 Pitt had persuaded parliament to agree to an establishment of 55,000 seamen for the navy. His opinion was that 'we ought to have our Navy as fully and as well manned as possible before we declare war'. The national debt funded such expenditure, increasing from £74 million to £133 million by the end of the war. Some 200,000 British families agreed to buy government bonds, tempted by the promise of interest payments funded from excise taxes charged on luxury goods such as tea, coffee, Indian cloth, and sugar. Such measures meant that in 1762 Britain possessed 120 ships of the line.

Despite the size of the Royal Navy, Spanish entry into the war made the philosopher Edmund Burke comment: 'Britain was never in such a doubtful and dangerous situation.' In theory, 50 Spanish ships of the line were now available to help the remaining 38 that remained in the French fleet after the twin defeats of Quiberon Bay and Basque Roads. However, with perhaps only 20 Spanish ships of the line immediately able to set sail, Spain was not ready to start major military operations. On 6 January, and only after hostilities had commenced, Ferrol, Cartagena, and Cadíz were ordered to equip 35 ships of the line for operations.

Havana was the exception. In peacetime the Armada de Barlovento normally consisted of two or three ships of the line, but in January 1762 a wartime establishment of 12 ships of the line was being maintained. On 29 June 1761 Admiral de Hevia and seven ships of the line arrived in the port, adding to the five already there. Hevia brought 996 men from the regiments of Spain and Aragon, bringing the garrison to 2,400 regulars, with 6,300 seamen, gunners, and marines aboard the ships. In addition there were three ships of the line at Santiago de Cuba, one at Vera Cruz, and three at Cartagena. From 1758 to 1761 Havana also received 153 cannon, 78,244 musket balls, over 40,000lb of gunpowder, and 5,000 muskets.

In Europe, Britain's numerical superiority in ships made the blockading of enemy ports possible. Nevertheless, if the French and Spanish navies could be concentrated either in home waters or in the colonies, it might still be feasible for them to take temporary command of the sea and carry out an amphibious operation against British shores or British colonies. Defensive precautions to keep the Spanish fleet from uniting with the French had already been made by reinforcing Admiral Saunders at Gibraltar. In November he suggested a raid on Cadíz to capture or destroy the ten Spanish ships of the line believed to be anchored in the bay; however, by 4 January the defences had been strengthened and ships withdrawn into the inner harbour; a raid was now impracticable and Saunders had to be satisfied with blockading the port. The British Ambassador in Madrid, Lord Bristol, also reported 11 ships of the line in Ferrol with orders to take 1,500 troops to the West Indies, but the belief in Britain was that a descent on Ireland was being threatened.

Four companies of the 2nd battalion of the 1st Royal Scots under Major Hamilton were sent to Havana (whether these included the grenadier company is unclear). From 1760–61 these companies had been fighting the Cherokee in the Carolinas. Their uniforms would probably have been modified to better suit tropical conditions. (Royal Scots Museum)

In the Caribbean, the British position benefited from decisions Pitt had made earlier in the year to send forces from England for another attempt on Martinique. In July Pitt had sent 7,000 Canadian veterans (11 battalions) under General Monckton from New York to the Caribbean for this very purpose. In September he added seven ships of the line to the 12 already there and placed Rear Admiral Rodney in charge. Another 3,000 men in four battalions (the 69th, 76th, 90th, and 98th), recently returned from the Belle Isle operation on the French coast, had also been ordered to the Caribbean. In early December all these decisions stood and the forces joined together at Barbados. However, there were still concerns for the safety of Jamaica, as a French squadron of eight ships of the line, four frigates, and 3,000 troops under Admiral Blenac had escaped from Brest on 23 December 1761. In January 1762, the Jamaican Governor warned Admiral Rodney of an invasion threat to his island, trying to prompt his recall from Martinique.

Back in London, the cabinet concluded that, under the current financial climate, a new, long-drawn-out naval war must be avoided. Prior to Spain's entry, the strategy had been to 'make the war in such a manner as we can maintain it longest'. Perhaps through necessity rather than design, the defeat of Spain would have to be the exception to this rule. The British needed the capture of Havana to be a swift, surprise blow, but on the continent the pursuit of a knockout blow (exemplified by Prussia and Austria) had been proven to be a fallacy. For them the tactics of annihilation had come to represent a strategy of exhaustion.

The Caribbean situation 1762

The operation against the French on Martinique proceeded with a landing on 16 January. Monckton had the same problems as Hopson with bringing up artillery. However, his larger force of 15 battalions made a more systematic approach possible, with batteries built 'to cover the troops in passing the gullies'. As at Guadeloupe, instead of landing in only one location, a series of smaller landings kept the defenders off balance and unable to concentrate in strength. St Pierre's harbour defences were captured from the landward side and on 15 February the island surrendered, Rodney writing that 'we are highly obliged to the inhabitants for their pusillanimous defence'. By then 1,800 British soldiers had either succumbed to disease or were unfit for duty.

Rodney then became aware of the hostilities with Spain. A Spanish order to seize all British ships was intercepted off Portugal by Captain Johnstone in the sloop *Hornet*. Johnstone sent his prize vessel to inform Rodney and it arrived two weeks before the official dispatch. A little later, on 5 March, Rodney received news of Blenac's escape from Brest. Approaching from windward, Blenac sailed to Martinique but, realizing the island had already fallen, then headed north. Rodney surmised that he was either sailing to the French port of Cape François on St Domingue or was trying to unite with the Spanish for a descent on Jamaica.

No such rendezvous occurred, and, observed by the sloop *Merlin*, Blenac sailed into Cape François on 15 March, losing the 64-gun *Dragon* aground on a sandbank in the process. Once there and conscious of the opportunity presented to him, he wrote to Prado in Havana, suggesting Hevia sail to Cape François as British ships close by could be easily surprised and destroyed; he then intimated they could take the offensive. But following convention and corresponding to Spanish notions of sea power, Prado and Hevia obeyed orders not to risk needless sorties. The prevailing winds were not in their favour. Whilst it was straightforward for the French to sail from St Domingue to Havana, for Hevia joining the French squadron at Cape François would require beating up against the wind.

Still conscious of the danger to Jamaica and with orders to go there if threatened, Rodney sent Commodore Douglas to the island with ten ships of the line. However, on 26 March the Admiral received orders to be ready with his whole squadron to unite with the expedition coming from England back at Martinique. He was told he was to be subordinate to the expedition's commander, Vice Admiral Pocock, but not of their destination. Rodney had a reputation for being difficult, a commander who was admired rather than liked. The threat to Jamaica led him to disobey his orders and he kept Douglas near the island, a decision the eminent naval historian J. S. Corbett judged as 'latitude of interpretation being stretched to its extreme limit'. Perhaps piqued about being made subordinate to Pocock, he also left Commodore Swanton with a squadron cruising the Spanish Main in search of prizes. Consequently, whilst Monckton's soldiers readied themselves for another operation, most of the ships allotted to be their naval escort had vanished. Anson's carefully planned sequence of events evolved in Whitehall over three months before was threatening to unravel.

Decisions taken in London

Back in January, Newcastle, although keen to avoid war with Spain, had ordered military chiefs to discuss 'the most effectual methods of distressing and attacking the Spaniards'. A secret committee of senior cabinet members, together with Anson and Ligonier, had therefore gathered in Horse Guards on 6 January for this purpose. An attendee, the Duke of Devonshire, reported

JANUARY 6 1762

Operation against Havana sanctioned

Pocock, aged 55, was immensely experienced, being familiar with the Caribbean from his time as commander-in-chief in the Leeward Islands during the War of Austrian Succession. More recently he had kept the French squadron in Mauritius from interfering with British operations against French possessions in India. (Anne SK Brown collection)

how the meeting started with consideration of 'Lord Anson's project of attacking Havannah'. According to Newcastle, after receiving confirmation from the military chiefs of 'the facility … there was in doing it', the cabinet approved the scheme. At the same meeting a plan by Colonel Draper (recently the chief of staff of the Belle Isle expedition) to use forces based in India to take Manila, the epicentre of Spain's Pacific trade, was also sanctioned. Follow-on operations against the Spanish in the Caribbean and the French in Louisiana were inferred, but not planned in detail.

The inspiration for the Havana operation stemmed from an intelligence report compiled by Admiral Knowles when, as Governor of Jamaica, he made an official visit to the city in 1756. Crucially, as he sailed into harbour, he was unable to see El Morro's landward defences and was therefore unaware of a sheer ditch on its landward side up to 70ft deep and over 20ft wide. His recommendation that taking El Morro was the best way to seize the city was therefore based on an inaccurate assessment of its defences.

Knowles was close to the Duke of Cumberland, George II's younger son. Cumberland had resigned in 1757 after leading the army in a disastrous campaign against the French in northern Germany, but was back in high regard as he was a favourite of the new King George III. In 1761, based on Knowles' report and recommendations, Cumberland proposed to attack the city and Pitt gave his support. Utilizing the mobility gained by movement by sea, a rapid descent against the centre of Spanish trade with its Empire was intended to paralyse the Spanish trading economy and force Spain to negotiate. The attack was not seen as an attempt to acquire a new permanent possession.

Contemporaries realized the scheme was ambitious. Cumberland wrote to his protégé Lord Albemarle: 'Any bystander would make me the projector of the expedition, but the truth is the subject is so tender, that I cannot allow even suppositions which are perhaps not quite groundless.' Perhaps there was reluctance to take responsibility for conceiving such an ambitious enterprise in case disaster struck. The cautious Newcastle favoured sending the regiments earmarked for Havana to Portugal instead, for although 7,000 men were already going to Lisbon, the Portuguese had requested more. He called the Havana expedition 'a most expensive, hazardous expedition … a wild goose chase', but was derided by the rest of the cabinet and planning for the expedition went ahead.

British commanders

Once the expedition had been approved, Anson and Ligonier had to select the commanders, needing men familiar with amphibious warfare and capable of acting together harmoniously. The experienced Vice-Admiral Pocock was chosen for overall command, with Commodore Augustus Keppel as his senior naval commander. Keppel had recently commanded the naval component at Belle Isle, in total 21 ships of the line. In order to make use of his experience of amphibious operations, his specific responsibility was to take charge of the arrangements for the landing. Another Keppel brother, William, was given one of the two divisional appointments which the size of the expedition merited, with the rank of acting major general. In 1747 Ligonier had noticed him in Flanders when both had been wounded and taken captive at the same battle. Lafausille was the other major general; he was Colonel of the 8th Foot, and had seized Île d'Aix in 1757.

George, the 3rd Earl of Albemarle and at 38 the oldest Keppel brother, was controversially appointed by the War Office to be the overall commander of the land forces. He had never held field command. Joining the Coldstream Guards at 14, since 1743 (at the age of 19) he had been a member of Cumberland's household and was his ADC at Fontenoy (1745) and Culloden (1746). Known to have a taste for extravagant uniforms, Albemarle was viewed by Wolfe as 'one of those showy men who are seen in places and the courts of men'. He nearly had a duel with Townshend, deputy to Wolfe at Quebec, after appearing to belittle his achievements; the encounter, which was already in motion, was stopped only by order of the king. Insecurity about his new appointment is perhaps indicated in a letter to General Amherst, the commanding officer in North America, after arriving in the Caribbean, when he wrote: 'Your officers are all generals, with a thorough contempt for everybody that had not served under Mr Wolfe; they either suffer, or cannot prevent, the soldiers doing what they please... I am greatly afraid they will oblige me to tell them my mind when we are better acquainted.'

Perhaps as a favour to his friend, Cumberland had persuaded the War Office to appoint Albemarle. A successful expedition would do much to re-establish the family fortune. Even if Albemarle's military talents were not yet proven, with all three brothers in senior appointments the relationship between the services, in contrast to the stormy relationship between Vernon and Wentworth at Cartagena in 1741, would give the Havana expedition the potential to be a model of command co-operation.

Albemarle's appointment was most likely due to his connections. His father was a general and Cumberland's right-hand man in the last war, but he had died in 1754 leaving practically nothing, despite being the British Ambassador in Paris. George II told Albemarle 'your father had a great many qualities but he was a sieve'. (Anne SK Brown collection)

In 1741 Keppel had served as a lieutenant on Anson's ship, the *Centurion*. In 1756 Anson gave him command of a new 74-gun ship, with which he took Gorée off the coast of Senegal in 1758 and sunk the *Thésée* during the Battle of Quiberon Bay in 1759. He would become the First Lord of the Admiralty in the 1780s. (Anne SK Brown collection)

Other senior command positions were filled by a constellation of rising stars. Colonel Carleton was the quartermaster general; he had been Wolfe's favourite, holding the same position at Quebec, and had commanded a brigade at Belle Isle. He would be placed in charge of a composite force of grenadiers and light infantry. Howe, the brother of the inspirational light infantry commander in North America killed at Ticonderoga in 1758, was the adjutant, but would be put in charge of an elite force of two grenadier battalions. (Howe and Carleton would both go on to fight in the American War of Independence). Elliot was the official second in command to Albemarle; in 1757 he had participated in raids on the French channel ports of Cherbourg and St Malo and would become the defender of Gibraltar in the 1780s. Two brigade commanders, Haviland and Rollo, both had experience of amphibious warfare in the Caribbean. Last but not least, Lieutenant Colonel Mackellar was the chief engineer, a post he had held at Quebec and Martinique. Officers for middle-ranking appointments were difficult to find as many realized the hazards that awaited them in the Caribbean; however, promotion could be expected as Albemarle, in expectation of losses from disease, was given authority to confer rank.

Spanish commanders

Field Marshal Don Juan de Prado, from 1761 the Governor of Havana, had previous prominence in Spanish circles, being a former inspector of the Spanish Infantry. He believed that the British would not 'even think of coming here as they cannot but be aware of our readiness to receive them'. The Conde de Superunda, José Antonio Manso de Velasco was commander of the army units at Havana, and the Marqués de Real de Transporte, Admiral Gutierre de Hevia, was the commander of the Spanish squadron. Baltasar Ricaud was the chief engineer, responsible for the state of the city's defences and José Crell the commander of the artillery. Colonel Arroyo was commander of the Regiment of Havana, which was based permanently in the city. But it was the middle-ranking officers that would rise from obscurity and be celebrated in years to come as the real defenders of Havana. A Spanish naval captain, Don Luis de Velasco of the ship *Reina* (70), would gain the respect of both sides for his defence of El Morro. His second in command was another naval captain, Marqués Gonzales, who had gained his title during an engagement with Admiral Mathews' squadron in 1744. The *Aquilón*, which was based permanently at Havana, was his first command of a ship of the line.

Havana Defences – Spanish Forces

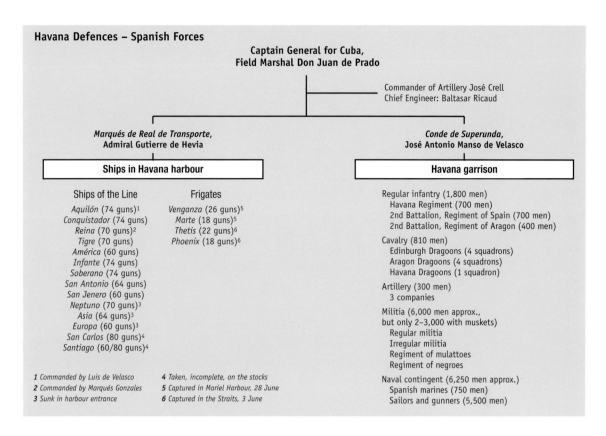

**Captain General for Cuba,
Field Marshal Don Juan de Prado**

Commander of Artillery José Crell
Chief Engineer: Baltasar Ricaud

Marqués de Real de Transporte,
Admiral Gutierre de Hevia

Conde de Superunda,
José Antonio Manso de Velasco

Ships in Havana harbour	Havana garrison

Ships of the Line
Aquilón (74 guns)[1]
Conquistador (74 guns)
Reina (70 guns)[2]
Tigre (70 guns)
América (60 guns)
Infante (74 guns)
Soberano (74 guns)
San Antonio (64 guns)
San Jenero (60 guns)
Neptuno (70 guns)[3]
Asia (64 guns)[3]
Europa (60 guns)[3]
San Carlos (80 guns)[4]
Santiago (60/80 guns)[4]

Frigates
Venganza (26 guns)[5]
Marte (18 guns)[5]
Thetis (22 guns)[6]
Phoenix (18 guns)[6]

Regular infantry (1,800 men)
Havana Regiment (700 men)
2nd Battalion, Regiment of Spain (700 men)
2nd Battalion, Regiment of Aragon (400 men)

Cavalry (810 men)
Edinburgh Dragoons (4 squadrons)
Aragon Dragoons (4 squadrons)
Havana Dragoons (1 squadron)

Artillery (300 men)
3 companies

**Militia (6,000 men approx.,
but only 2–3,000 with muskets)**
Regular militia
Irregular militia
Regiment of mulattoes
Regiment of negroes

Naval contingent (6,250 men approx.)
Spanish marines (750 men)
Sailors and gunners (5,500 men)

1 *Commanded by Luis de Velasco*
2 *Commanded by Marqués Gonzales*
3 *Sunk in harbour entrance*
4 *Taken, incomplete, on the stocks*
5 *Captured in Mariel Harbour, 28 June*
6 *Captured in the Straits, 3 June*

As a junior officer in the 1730s, Velasco had battled corsairs in the Mediterranean. When serving as a frigate commander in the Caribbean in 1741, he took a larger British frigate and a brigantine through boarding in one engagement, and in 1746 he captured a 36-gun frigate. He stayed in Cuba and in 1754 was given the 70-gun *Reina*. (Museo Naval Madrid)

THE PLAN

The Havana plan was ambitious: to assemble 16,000 troops from three locations – Britain, the Caribbean, and New York – for an amphibious assault against a well-defended fortress city. It was a race against time as the hurricane season began in August, and the operation required the co-ordination of large numbers of troops, ships, and supplies from widely disparate theatres to achieve strategic surprise and apply decisive force at a single critical point.

A comparatively small force of 4,000 men in four regiments (the 22nd, 34th, 56th, and 72nd) plus a Royal Artillery detachment and seven engineers selected by the Board of Ordnance would be sent from England. Most of the assaulting force, numbering 8,000 or so under the command of General Monckton, was already in the Caribbean fighting for possession of Martinique. Another 4,000 men made up of British regulars and American provincials in equal measure were to be dispatched from North America.

Albemarle was given discretion on how to capture Havana. On 15 February he was ordered 'to make the most vigorous attack ... and exert your utmost endeavours to make yourself master of Havana'. The dangers of a protracted siege, in terms of the losses to be expected from disease, encouraged aggression. An immediate storming of the city would, one way or the other, offer a quick conclusion to affairs. However, Albemarle hinted at a cautionary approach when he wrote to Amherst how the Canadian veterans 'have conquered in a few days the strongest country you ever saw [Martinique], in the American way – running, or with the Indian hoop [whoop]' and he considered 'that manner of fighting will not always succeed and I dread their meeting troops that will stand their ground. They are certainly brave and will be cut to pieces.'

Conscious of the rivalry that blighted operations at Cartagena, Albemarle was told 'to cultivate good understanding and agreement' with the naval officers, as 'the success of this expedition will very much depend on an entire good understanding between our land and sea officers'. Cumberland, wise to the need for haste, also provided advice, counselling 'dear Albemarle, get away as fast as you can'. In case a naval bombardment was contemplated, he also felt necessary to write: 'I gave your brother [Augustus] false intelligence about the Morro fort, for he asked whether ships could anchor before the Fort, and I answered in the negative, but on further enquiry of Knowles, he says the men of war may anchor as near as they please in from 4–6 fathoms of water, though he had assured me he had told your brother, yet I thought it safest to write you myself.' As an aside he referred to Knowles who was 'croaking every day at dinner'.

On 5 February Lord Egremont, the Southern Secretary, had issued orders for Monckton on Martinique, informing him that the goal was to be Havana and 'all other enterprises will yield to this objective'. If Martinique had not yet been taken, Monckton should leave a force sufficient to retain possession of those forts that had been captured on the island and rendezvous with Pocock on Dominica or St Lucia (which had already been seized from the French). If Martinique had fallen, however, Monckton was to wait for Pocock's convoy, expected to arrive in mid-April, and was given the choice to either proceed with his men to Havana or remain as governor with the regiments from Belle Isle as his garrison.

In his orders of 18 February, Pocock was similarly told to conduct 'the most vigorous attack' and 'exert your most utmost endeavours' to capture Havana. He was to take out the *Namur*, *Valiant*, *Hampton Court*, *Orford*, *Edgar*, *Belle-Isle*, and *Mercury*, along with 18 transports 'laden with provisions for 16,000 men over seven months'. In addition, 32 troop transports just returned from Belle Isle were unloaded and cleaned in three weeks for his use. Once united with Monckton in the Caribbean, he was given permission to pay for more transports as required and the Admiralty told him that the 'utmost expedition must be used' in loading them.

Pocock was then to sail via Cape St Nicholas in St Domingue, where he was to be joined by the North American convoy, and 'proceed with them through the Old Straits of Bahama to the Havana on the island of Cuba'. The word Bahamas is from the Spanish *baja mar*, meaning low water, and the Straits are a narrow channel 100 miles long between the Bahamas and Cuba that had been marked on an old Spanish chart Anson gave Pocock. The sloop *Bonetta* from New Providence would deliver local pilots for this potentially treacherous journey. Normally, ships sailing to Havana would pass around the western tip of Cuba and beat 200 miles back upwind, which would have given the Spanish plenty of warning of their arrival. The unexpected approach down the channel was designed to take the Spanish by surprise. If the North Americans failed to make the rendezvous, Pocock was ordered to proceed without them.

On 5 February orders had also gone out to Admiral Rodney. To embark Monckton's men at Martinique he was to 'cause 16,000 tons of transports to be provided and fitted out for 8,000 men and victualled for 3 months'. Crucially, he was also to 'cause such ten ships of the line … to be likewise victualled and stored and put into condition ready to proceed upon further service'. Interestingly, the Admiralty told him only that the expedition was to make 'some signal and effectual impression on the Spanish colonies in the West Indies'. Aware of his prickly temperament, the Admiralty pressed compliance by saying it was 'unnecessary to add any motives to enforce the

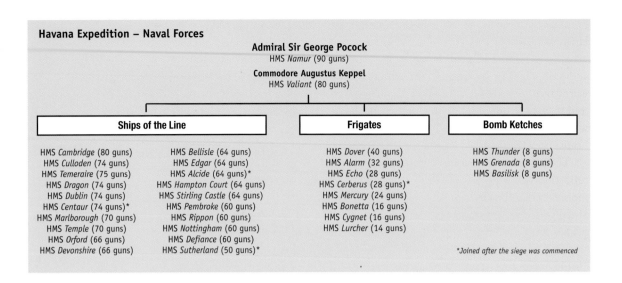

Havana Expedition – Naval Forces

Admiral Sir George Pocock
HMS *Namur* (90 guns)

Commodore Augustus Keppel
HMS *Valiant* (80 guns)

Ships of the Line	Frigates	Bomb Ketches
HMS *Cambridge* (80 guns) HMS *Bellisle* (64 guns)	HMS *Dover* (40 guns)	HMS *Thunder* (8 guns)
HMS *Culloden* (74 guns) HMS *Edgar* (64 guns)	HMS *Alarm* (32 guns)	HMS *Grenada* (8 guns)
HMS *Temeraire* (75 guns) HMS *Alcide* (64 guns)*	HMS *Echo* (28 guns)	HMS *Basilisk* (8 guns)
HMS *Dragon* (74 guns) HMS *Hampton Court* (64 guns)	HMS *Cerberus* (28 guns)*	
HMS *Dublin* (74 guns) HMS *Stirling Castle* (64 guns)	HMS *Mercury* (24 guns)	
HMS *Centaur* (74 guns)* HMS *Pembroke* (60 guns)	HMS *Bonetta* (16 guns)	
HMS *Marlborough* (70 guns) HMS *Rippon* (60 guns)	HMS *Cygnet* (16 guns)	
HMS *Temple* (70 guns) HMS *Nottingham* (60 guns)	HMS *Lurcher* (14 guns)	
HMS *Orford* (66 guns) HMS *Defiance* (60 guns)		
HMS *Devonshire* (66 guns) HMS *Sutherland* (50 guns)*		

Joined after the siege was commenced

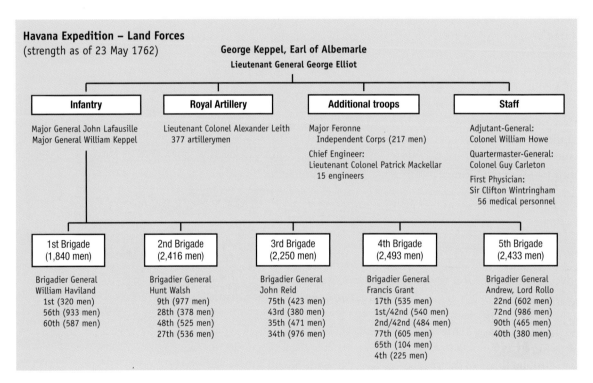

Havana Expedition – Land Forces
(strength as of 23 May 1762)

George Keppel, Earl of Albemarle
Lieutenant General George Elliot

Infantry	Royal Artillery	Additional troops	Staff
Major General John Lafausille Major General William Keppel	Lieutenant Colonel Alexander Leith 377 artillerymen	Major Feronne Independent Corps (217 men)	Adjutant-General: Colonel William Howe
		Chief Engineer: Lieutenant Colonel Patrick Mackellar 15 engineers	Quartermaster-General: Colonel Guy Carleton
			First Physician: Sir Clifton Wintringham 56 medical personnel

1st Brigade (1,840 men)	2nd Brigade (2,416 men)	3rd Brigade (2,250 men)	4th Brigade (2,493 men)	5th Brigade (2,433 men)
Brigadier General William Haviland	Brigadier General Hunt Walsh	Brigadier General John Reid	Brigadier General Francis Grant	Brigadier General Andrew, Lord Rollo
1st (320 men)	9th (977 men)	75th (423 men)	17th (535 men)	22nd (602 men)
56th (933 men)	28th (378 men)	43rd (380 men)	1st/42nd (540 men)	72nd (986 men)
60th (587 men)	48th (525 men)	35th (471 men)	2nd/42nd (484 men)	90th (465 men)
	27th (536 men)	34th (976 men)	77th (605 men)	40th (380 men)
			65th (104 men)	
			4th (225 men)	

most punctual and expeditious obedience … we therefore rely on your hearty concurrence'. The Jamaica station was ordered to call in its six ships of the line and victual them for four months, also in preparation for joining Pocock.

Whether the attack on Havana had been successful or not, Albemarle and Pocock were told to undertake further operations. Albemarle was to choose either 'La Vera Cruz, Pensacola, St Augustine, Santiago de Cuba, or any other part of the Spanish colonies … you shall judge to be most practicable'. Additionally, the force from North America was to be detached, along with any units Albemarle thought he could spare, to participate in an attack on

Louisiana, the last French possession on the North American continent. However, half of these troops were provincials and, despite ordering Albemarle 'to take especial care that they may be treated with all such proper attention and humanity', these plans did not consider the limitation of service provincials were given, namely that they signed up for only one campaign. Albemarle was told to ensure 'they may be induced readily and cheerfully to act in conjunction with the regular forces on any further occasion', but diverting them to Louisiana rather than returning them home would have blighted relations.

The British use of provincials in the Seven Years War deserves further reflection because of the emphasis Pitt placed on utilizing them. He found it increasingly difficult to recruit men in Britain, which was only in part ameliorated by the passing of a Recruiting Act designed to press 'idle able bodied men' into service and a Militia Act to raise troops for the defence of the country. In 1758 colonial assemblies were given £1 million to arm and clothe provincials, and 22,500 signed on. Expanding the employment of provincials can be seen to be counterproductive, however, for the men were recruited for specific campaigns; once over, they would go home to their families. Also, the pool of men in America from which regular regiments could recruit was reduced. While 15,500 regulars went to North America from 1755 to 1757, only 3,000 in 1758 and 2,000 in 1760 came from Britain as replacement drafts. Regiments were soon 7,000 men under establishment. Furthermore, provincials could not perform the role of regulars. They were not supposed to assault a landing beach or storm a fortress. Support functions such as construction of roads and entrenchments, moving supplies, and manning defences – all integral to siege operations – were their primary function. Some regular North American colonial units were at Havana, notably the 60th Royal American Regiment, established in 1756, with four battalions, one of which went with Monckton to the Caribbean.

Mackellar's memorandum

In a memorandum he wrote for the expedition's commanding officers, Lieutenant Colonel Mackellar considered the best approach for capturing

Ships storming the narrow harbour entrance would have been raked by Spanish ships and targeted by this battery at the foot of El Morro called the 'Twelve Apostles'. La Punta, situated at sea level, can be seen on the other side of the harbour entrance.

Mante noted the ditch's dimensions: by the sea bastion the depth was approximately 63ft 4in and the width 56ft; along the curtain wall the depth was 56ft 6in but the width 105ft; and by the landward bastion the depth was 45ft and the width 43ft 4in. In addition the bastions were raised 25ft above the rock.

Havana. He thought a move down the harbour entrance to land men directly into the city unadvisable, but did not presume siege operations would be required – advising that a rapid assault could be conducted by a force landed on the west side, but only if 'the garrison is too weak or does not exceed one quarter or one fifth of the besieging army'. He signalled out the weakest spot in the walls to assault as 'the most advanced bastion, which is the fourth from La Punta, and against its collateral bastion on the right', these being more out of sight of the other bastions, El Morro, and the harbour. Mackellar recognized that El Morro dominated both the town and La Punta; however, he disagreed with Knowles' overriding attachment to its importance, stating the Admiral's 'reasons for doing so are not very full' and that the 'only reason' why it was important was the 'command of the ground of La Punta' it offered.

If siege operations were to be carried out, Mackellar thought there was still a decision to be made about whether to land to the east or the west of the harbour as 'landing on both sides … is perhaps inconsistent with our force'. Both sides had nearby anchorages for ships to land stores, to the west at Chorera and to the east at Cojimar, and both had gently sloping beaches to land the men. The factors influencing the choice of locations were 'where approaches may be least annoyed, the ground that yields the most command, the nearest cover, and [is] the easiest to work, and that where the artillery and the materials for the works of the siege can be brought with the least trouble and fatigue'. On the east side Mackellar recognized the vital ground: 'La Cabaña, or Stone Quarry Hills, command the town, a considerable part of the harbour, and El Morro, and have space enough for erecting batteries.' (These heights had not been substantially fortified by the Spanish and began only 400yds from El Morro). Furthermore, he surmised that the Spanish coming either from the town or El Morro would find conducting sorties against the siege works difficult; disengaging from such sallies and re-embarking on boats to regain the city would also be fraught with danger. A British camp located on a wooded slope on a narrow headland could be easily defended and would not be vulnerable to cavalry – advantages that did not apply on the more gently sloping ground to the west of the town.

Two other important factors for the siege works related to the environment: the nature of the soil and the availability of fresh water. The soil on the west side was known to be rocky and therefore not conducive to siege operations, but Mackellar correctly predicted it would be little better on the east side. The west side had a water supply, 'a rivulet of water … runs in branches into the town', but 'there was no account of any water on the side of El Morro'. Another important factor he highlighted was that Chorera would be a further 4½ miles away from siege works built against the town than Cojimar would be from those constructed against El Morro. However, a look at the map shows that he was mistaken in his assumption that Chorera was closer to Havana's walls than Cojimar was to El Morro's. His error could have tipped the balance in favour of Cojimar.

Mackellar, because he was unaware of the existence of the ditch on its landward side, presumed El Morro weaker than was actually the case. He was also unsure whether the city walls had 'outworks, ditches or covered way' and listed this as an information requirement. Other questions remained: the availability of water at Cojimar, the nature of the soil on that side, and whether the town's ramparts were entirely of masonry or filled with clay. However, on balance he favoured the east side for siege operations.

From the information available to him, Mackellar presented Albemarle with, on the whole, an objective assessment of the advantages and disadvantages of the various approaches to capture Havana. He had not discussed a timetable for the siege or mentioned the expected effects of the climate; perhaps these were implicit in his memo, which he probably intended as a technical paper only. No records have been found to suggest when Albemarle made up his mind which plan to adopt; however, aware of the dangers, and with no field command under his belt, he was more likely drawn to the more methodical and acknowledged option of taking El Morro first. Once closer to Havana, more intelligence might become available to further inform his decision.

Landing from the sea: procedures, equipment and experience

Major Grant, the marine detachment commander on HMS *Rippon*, wrote 'of all species of warfare that of landing is the most unpleasant [as] you present a mark for your enemy and you are not in your element'. Soldiers disembarking from boats on a hostile shore were vulnerable. They took time to form up to deploy their firepower effectively, and for a time did not have the security of their own ranks. Thomas Molyneaux, author of the book *Conjunct Expeditions* in 1759, drew attention to the consequences of using different boats of shape and size 'drawing several depths of water, consequently requiring different time to gain the same space ... almost sure of not arriving at the destined place together'. The result was that 'at our debarkments, it is true we debark an Army, but we never yet debarked regiments. At the very moment the Army is required to be in regiments most, it is least.'

Efforts had recently been made to improve procedures. In 1757 during the landing at Rochefort, Hawke tried to ensure boats carrying the same units were kept together, and ordered all naval officers 'to range their boats in divisions, and in such a manner that every regiment may be all together'. At Havana the intention was to form up and march on important locations around the city before the Spanish could rouse a defence. If storming the town was not possible then locations to build batteries would have to be taken. The outer works and then the city walls had to be reduced before tropical disease decimated the army. New longboats, measuring 38ft in length and 11ft in

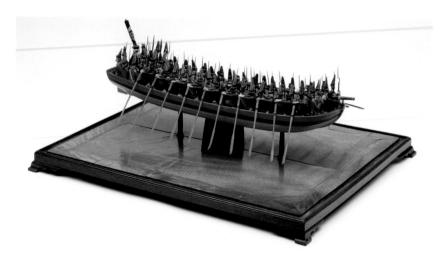

breadth, could approach the shore more closely than any other rowing boat because of their shallow draft. They were specialized landing craft of a standard size, carried on the decks of landing ships that were hoisted overboard when required. The boats were crewed by an officer and 20 seamen, each pulling an oar, and could facilitate a quick and orderly disembarkation.

In February 1762, after having seen the regiments going to Havana loaded onto transports at Portsmouth, the Hanoverian Count Kielmansegge described in his diary how the longboats 'accelerated the embarkation and disembarkation of troops'. Upon a signal 'each officer marched with his men to the boat, of which he had previously recorded the number; then he and his drummer entered first and passed right through the bows on shore to the stern, the whole division following without breaking their ranks; so that in two minutes everyone was in the boat'. Each man knew the part he was going to play, for 'the officers and drummer, with their corporals, sit aft near the rudder, the privates in two or three rows behind one another on the thwarts, holding their muskets before them, and two petty officers in the bow, but the oarsmen occupy special rows between the soldiers, and a little in front of them, so as not to be hampered in the use of the oars'.

Procedures for landing troops from these boats on hostile shores were being developed. John MacIntire, a lieutenant in the Royal Marines, wrote a treatise on marine forces in 1763 and noted how troops were ordered to have 'the flints good and well screwed in, the bayonet fixed properly, and the rammers well fitted, taking care that every soldier carries with him a screw driver, a worm, two good flints, besides the one in his piece, forty rounds of ammunition and a day's dry provisions in case of accidents'. Modifications were carried out to weapons. Leather or cloth covers were put over priming pans, and equipment was slung over the shoulder rather than around the waist, all in order to keep it dry. Furthermore, when the men plunged into the surf, soldiers 'must hold their firelocks high recovered, to preserve their shot, keeping their ammunition from the wet'. Marines even wore special sugarloaf-shaped hats to make it easier to sling their musket.

Marines actually represented only a small percentage of the force that was landed. At Cartagena six out of eight regiments put ashore were titled marines, but these men were marines in name only; the previous year the men were recruited into army regiments that had their designation changed. More typically they formed part of the complement of a warship and had specialized roles, including a function that would be carried out at Havana and described by MacIntire, namely 'to attack a small fort on the landside, when a ship is battering it from the sea'.

During a landing, naval gunfire support could be given by ships firing from the flanks. At Fort Louis on Guadeloupe, Highlanders and marines landing on an entrenched beach were supported in this way. The navy also developed the use of bomb ketches, sturdy vessels built with heavy frames and beams capable of carrying mortars that could fire a shell 2–3 miles. The shells could be explosive or incendiary, the latter composed of sulphur, nitre, as well as gunpowder, to set fire to urban areas. The fuse was cut by the gunners, which meant shells could explode in mid-air. These weapons were used on the night of 16 January 1759 to destroy Basse-Terre on Guadeloupe, a vindictive act as no assault followed on from the bombardment.

Many units and their commanders had recent experience of amphibious landings in Europe, North America, and the Caribbean. From 1758 Pitt had been keen to divert French forces from Germany and, encouraged by merchant interest groups, directed that landings be made on the French coast. Cherbourg and St Malo were both successfully raided and large quantities of naval stores used by privateers were destroyed. In April 1761 the operation against Belle Isle, an island 15 miles long by 5 miles wide that lay off the Brittany coast (as far as the Isle of Wight is from Portsmouth), started in failure. The initial landing was aborted with the loss of most of the troops put ashore. A second, unexpected attempt by grenadiers and marines on a rocky shore in fog was surprisingly successful, in part as 'men were squatting upon their backsides to reload which saved them from the enemy shot'. By the end of the first day 900 men had established a bridgehead, which, when reinforced, eventually sealed the fate of the 4,000-strong garrison.

In North America, the capture through siege of Louisbourg in 1758 was possible only after a landing on an entrenched beach in nearby Gabarus Bay. Richard Humphrys described in his journal how 'nothing was seen or heard for one hour but the thundering of cannon and flashes of lightning'. A year later at Quebec, the men landed silently at night and scaled a steep cliff, much to the surprise of the French, and prompted them to injudiciously leave the safety of the city's walls in an effort to throw the British back into the river.

In the Caribbean, the dangers of landing on foreign, unfamiliar territory also became apparent. In 1759 the attempt to take Martinique ran into trouble because of the close terrain of the interior. Martinique's jagged coastline has 300ft cliffs rising almost perpendicularly from the sea, and its mountainous interior with peaks rising over 5,000ft, riven with deep ravines, in 1762 was covered with tropical forest and thick thorns, and dotted with cane plantations. For French irregulars sniping and ambushing from concealed and often entrenched positions, this camouflage country was so perfect a deserter complained he 'found no enemy to fight'. In 1762 on the same island, the British needed to be held at constant readiness in order to repel sudden attacks, even during periods of rest back in camp. Strict discipline was enforced to keep the men straying from the beaten path, and as the historian Brumwell surmised, 'operations ... presented more problems to the provost rather than the tacticians'.

Spanish preparations at Havana

Preparations the Spanish Government made for war after signing the compact with France focused more on Portugal than the colonies. As already seen, there was a lack of planning for any combined French–Spanish action in the Caribbean theatre. Prado underestimated the British threat to his island, and Hevia was keen to keep his fleet safe in port. Although Prado's orders from Madrid informing him of the declaration of war were intercepted when the *Milford* boarded a Spanish *aviso* (dispatch boat), by 26 February he knew hostilities had commenced, even if British plans remained a mystery. Prado believed in the impregnability of Havana, and wanted a transfer to Florida where he thought there was more chance of combat. Confident that with Hevia's ships he was strong enough to repel any British attack, he joked with the king that he hoped the British would come as defeat would dissuade them from attacking any other Spanish base. He was lulled into a false sense of security because the British concentration was effected at Martinique rather than Jamaica, which was more easily observed from Cuba. Although he knew Martinique had fallen, not enough effort was made to collect intelligence on the future destination of the British expedition.

There is some debate amongst Spanish historians about the strength of the Spanish armed forces at Havana. In the 1850s, Guiteras estimated 3,000 regulars were present and Pezuela put the figure at around 2,000. The regiments of Havana, Spain, and Aragon certainly comprised the regular units of the garrison. There were also nine squadrons of cavalry from the Havana, Aragon, and Edinburgh dragoon regiments, and three companies of artillery. A large body of militia were available, given as 6,432 men by the historian McNeill in the 1990s, but according to Pezuela they were grossly under-equipped with only 2,000 muskets available to them.

Though El Morro was a formidable fortress, Spanish commanders were concerned the guns mainly faced the bay and port, and were conscious of the threat from La Cabaña. Francisco Ricaud had been in charge of fortifying La Cabaña, but in October 1761 he died of yellow fever and Baltasar took over. Building work was very slow because of the lack of personnel assigned to the task and by the end of 1761 platforms for only seven cannon had been constructed.

Hevia's 12 ships of the line were in Havana Harbour with 5,000–6,000 sailors and 750 marines, but N. A. M. Rodger suggests they were 'unrigged as though laid up for winter'. Pocock's approach through the Old Bahama Channel was intended to be unobserved and give the Spanish no reason to stir. However, Blenac was capable of interfering with the progress of the British fleet to Havana and any supply or subsequent reinforcement of the expedition once it had landed.

APPROACH AND LANDING

The approach

In London that February, Horace Walpole wrote how gossip was of 'a mighty expedition on the point of sailing' but 'whose destination is not disclosed'. Pocock left for Portsmouth on the 15th, followed soon after by Anson with a party of visiting dignitaries (including Count Kielmansegge). Over the next few days, four regiments paraded on Southsea Common before boarding flat-bottomed boats to take them to their transports at Spithead. The dignitaries were taken on Pocock's flagship *Namur* for a final farewell prior to the fleet's departure. On 5 March five ships of the line, one frigate, and 67 other sail, with their yards manned and to a thumping salute, left Portsmouth and sailed past the Isle of Wight to catch an easterly breeze to take them down the English Channel and from there to the broad seas of the Atlantic.

Archibald Robertson, a young engineer from Edinburgh, described in his diary how on 12 March a thick fog descended so that his ship lost sight of the fleet; on 20 March a violent storm in the Atlantic caused one transport to lose its topmast and another its mizzenmast. After this, fair winds took the fleet to Carlisle Bay in Barbados, arriving on 20 April. During the passage only five transports had been separated from the fleet and they quickly caught up.

Before reaching the Caribbean, Pocock had been informed by a dispatch from Rodney, written on 31 March, that Martinique had fallen and that Commodore Douglas had been sent to Jamaica with ten sail of the line, for 'I was informed … the Spaniards intended to attack that island.' Touching Barbados but briefly, he sailed to Martinique where the fleet watered on 26 April. Once there he had to write to Rodney, who was too ill to meet him, asking for all the intelligence gathered on the threat to Jamaica and the dispositions of the ships under his command. He commandeered Rodney's flagship, the *Marlborough*, and ordered Douglas at Jamaica to join him on 12 May at Cape St Nicholas (off the west tip of Hispaniola, only 50 miles from the French base at Cape François) with the words: 'Nothing is to

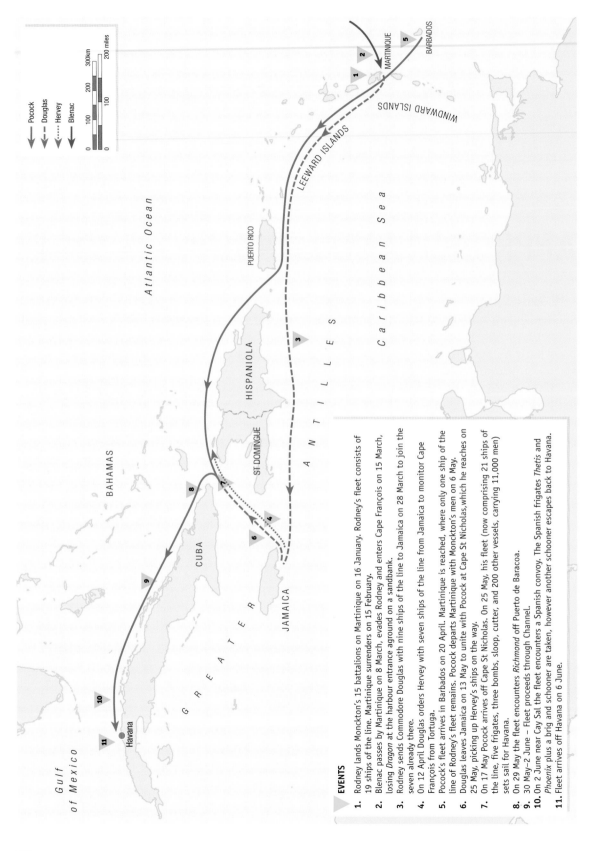

EVENTS

1. Rodney lands Monckton's 15 battalions on Martinique on 16 January. Rodney's fleet consists of 19 ships of the line.

2. Blenac passes by Martinique on 8 March, evades Rodney and enters Cape François on 15 March, losing *Dragon* at the harbour entrance aground on a sandbank.

3. Rodney sends Commodore Douglas with nine ships of the line to Jamaica on 28 March to join the seven ships already there.

4. On 12 April Douglas orders Hervey with seven ships of the line from Jamaica to monitor Cape François from Tortuga.

5. Pocock's fleet arrives in Barbados on 20 April. Martinique is reached, where only one ship of the line of Rodney's fleet remains. Pocock departs Martinique with Monckton's men on 6 May.

6. Douglas leaves Jamaica on 13 May to unite with Pocock at Cape St Nicholas, which he reaches on 25 May, picking up Hervey's ships on the way.

7. On 17 May Pocock arrives off Cape St Nicholas. On 25 May, his fleet (now comprising 21 ships of the line, five frigates, three bombs, sloop, cutter, and 200 other vessels, carrying 11,000 men) sets sail for Havana.

8. On 29 May the fleet encounters *Richmond* off Puerto de Baracoa.

9. 30 May–2 June – Fleet proceeds through Channel.

10. On 2 June near Cay Sal the fleet encounters a Spanish convoy. The Spanish frigates *Thetis* and *Phoenix* plus a brig and schooner are taken, however another schooner escapes back to Havana.

11. Fleet arrives off Havana on 6 June.

prevent you immediately proceeding to join me but the island of Jamaica's being actually attacked by a considerable force of the enemy's.'

Pocock found himself delayed at Martinique, however. Monckton had already embarked 8,000 men on transports, but Albemarle discovered the men had been permitted to take 'what transports they liked, or such as they could get'. Showing an awareness of proper landing procedures, he ordered the whole army to be re-embarked. A system of different flags indicated which regiment each of the transports carried. Only on 6 May did the fleet, now composed of 156 ships divided into red, blue, and white divisions, leave Martinique. Monckton, in bad health, was given permission to return to New York. A trade convoy bound for Jamaica and two further ships of the line joined the fleet at St Kitts. The route then took the fleet to the north of Hispaniola, skirting the northern shore of French St Domingue, and into potential danger.

Douglas had not been idle at Jamaica. On his own initiative he sent Captain Hervey with seven ships of the line to watch Blenac. Whilst Hervey with most of his ships had returned to Jamaica to take on provisions and stores, Pocock passed Cape François and was informed the French Admiral was still there. Pocock continued and reached the rendezvous at Cape St Nicholas on 17 May, but had to wait until the 25th before Hervey and Douglas arrived. Only at this juncture did Pocock achieve an overwhelming force, composed of 20 ships of the line. The delay caused Robertson to surmise the destination of the expedition was St Domingue: 'The flat bottomed boats being ordered aboard the men of war and signals being hoisted out from the Admiral for the Majors of Brigade, etc we imagined we were going to land.' His thoughts seemed to confirm an article written in the *London Gazette* in February that this was the objective of the expedition.

**MARCH 5
1762**

**Fleet sets
sail from
Portsmouth**

During the night, at either side of the most dangerous part of the channel (between Cay Lobos and Cayo Confites), bonfires were lit on reefs that broke the surface, which according to the Journal 'reconciled everyone to the dangers and risk of so hazardous an undertaking'. This is a section of the Elphinston chart showing the channel from Cay Lobos (point D on the chart) to Cay Sal. (Naval Historical Branch)

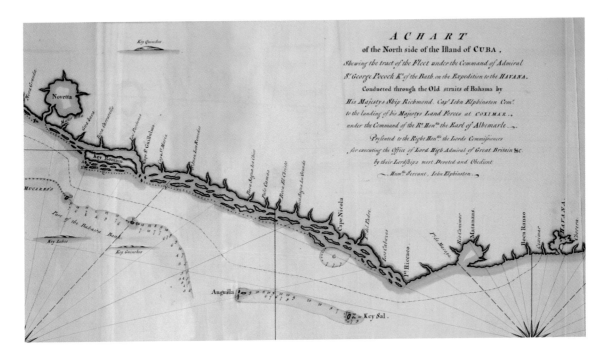

33

More by coincidence rather than intention, the Spanish and French were perhaps similarly fooled.

On 26 May Pocock heard from New York that the Americans had been delayed and were only just ready to sail; there was no point in waiting for them. The next day the trade fleet with Douglas in the *Centurion* parted company for Jamaica. On the 28th Cuba was sighted, and the following day Captain Elphinston in the *Richmond* rejoined the fleet having been sent by Douglas to make a survey of the channel as far as Cay Sal. Elphinston had been diligent and Anson's captured Spanish chart was shown to be accurate.

The fleet prepared to make its most hazardous voyage and was divided into seven formations for the passage, each identified by a separate pennant. The channel was entered on 30 May, Elphinston at first keeping ahead to lead the rest through because the pilots from New Providence were found wanting. Pocock was in the van with four ships of the line, six more were strung through the centre and a total of nine covered the rear in case Blenac made an appearance.

The approach of the fleet down the channel would be visible on shore but no messenger on land could go faster than the fleet. Enemy naval vessels would be another matter, however. On 2 June the frigates *Alarm* and *Echo* sent to lie on the Cay Sal bank sighted five sail: the Spanish frigate *Thetis*, the armed store ship *Phoenix*, and three smaller vessels, all part of a convoy from Havana to collect timber for the shipyard. The *Alarm* and *Echo* engaged the *Thetis* and *Phoenix* for over 30 minutes and forced them to strike their colours. A brig and a schooner were also taken, but the remaining schooner escaped back up the channel to take news of the British fleet to Havana. A captured Spanish officer of the *Thetis* revealed the Spanish at Havana had '14 men-of-war of the line', and, according to Pocock, Albemarle was given a correct appreciation of the strength of the garrison, which would have encouraged him to make a landing to the east of the harbour. On the evening of 5 June, the fleet safely passed Cay Sal and was clear of the straits; next morning, a Sunday, Havana was only 15 miles off the port bow.

Arrangements for the landing

Carleton and Howe went on board the frigates *Richmond* and *Alarm* to make a reconnaissance of the beaches to the east of the city. However, that same day Captain Hervey advised Pocock that the west side 'appears to be a very fine coast, cleared and very easy for a descent, level to the town, and not the least obstruction to any approaches'. He believed a sudden attack from this side might succeed. Albemarle had to make a decision and preferred formal siege operations rather than a risky assault. He could not ignore the importance of the heights of La Cabaña south of El Morro, as batteries mounted here could dominate the harbour and the city. El Morro it would be, but to guard against a possible attack from the interior, a 'considerable large village' called Guanabacoa (an important crossroads on rising ground to the south-east) would be captured first.

Commodore Augustus Keppel was appointed to take charge of the landing operation and Pocock gave him seven ships of the line, several frigates, and all the troop transports. In the afternoon Pocock sailed to Chorera, 4 miles west of the city, with 13 ships of the line, two frigates, and all the 36 store and supply ships to convince the Spanish the main landing would be made there.

Pocock's general instructions for the landing of troops had been laid out in articles written whilst he was sailing off Hispaniola on 16 May. A series of signals for every eventuality were mandated: either flags, or lights and gunshots for night-time, all to ensure landing boats could be directed as necessary by the Admiral or their naval division commanders, whether it be to postpone an operation, embark in the flat-bottomed boats, row towards the shore, or change direction. Signal flags or lights would also indicate the success or otherwise of the landing.

The articles specified each flat-bottomed boat was to be rowed by 16 oarsmen, with a good petty officer to steer and a midshipman to command. If surf was present onshore, the midshipman must be 'sure to drop the boat's grapnel, that he may be able to haul the boat off by it'. Whilst the seamen would assist the soldiers 'as much as possible in getting in and out of the boats', the midshipmen were to ensure 'not to allow more than two bowmen [sailors at the bow end of the boat] to get out of the boats upon landing' because once the soldiers disembarked, the boats were to immediately return to the transports 'to take on board as many troops as he can conveniently carry'. On 6 June Pocock issued these instructions to the captains and masters of transports, and ordered all the flat-bottomed boats to be hoisted overboard.

Prado's reaction

On the morning of Sunday 6 June, the garrison of Cojimar was the first to spot Pocock's fleet. The fort's commandant, Gabriel Subiera, sent a messenger to Prado who was woken and taken to El Morro; but he thought it was a trade convoy sailing east that had passed Havana during the night, and attended mass in the cathedral to celebrate Pentecost. Subiera refuted this assumption but only in the afternoon, when Pocock sailed past the harbour to Chorera, did Prado change his mind. A council of war was hastily convened and a force of infantry and cavalry under Colonel Don Carlos Caro was ordered to Chorera. A larger force of regular infantry and cavalry with a militia contingent was sent to Guanabacoa to stop any troops landing on the east side moving around the harbour to attack the city from the west. In order to protect the fully laden merchant ships in the harbour, he ordered the sinking of three ships of the line in the entrance, which occurred on 8, 9 and 10 June, and the construction of a boom, which was put in place on the 9th. To inform other garrisons that Havana was under attack, messengers were quickly dispatched to all parts of Cuba.

Hevia persuaded the war council to deploy his sailors and marines to the fortifications and replace garrison commanders with naval captains. Velasco was appointed commander of El Morro garrison with Marqués Gonzales as his second in command. Captain Briceño was sent to take command of La Punta. Prado, realizing the importance of La Cabaña heights, ordered 1,000 sailors to make a hurried attempt to haul up some guns to the platforms.

**JUNE 6
1762**

**Fleet arrives
15 miles off
Havana**

He was confident of holding El Morro as it could easily be reinforced from the harbour. Despite ordering the evacuation of all the women and children (which spread panic and resulted in civilians clogging the streets) he predicted the British would be laid low by yellow fever within two months.

The landing

The beach chosen for the landing, identified by Knowles, was a 3-mile stretch of shore between the Cojimar and Bacuranao Rivers that gave way to a wooded slope. Knowles had noted a small fort at the mouth of each of these rivers, the first with eight or ten guns and the second with five or six, which he inferred could both be quickly silenced. Keppel had the *Valiant*, *Dragon*, *Temeraire*, *Orford*, *Pembroke*, *Rippon*, *Dover*, *Richmond*, *Trent*, *Mercury*, *Bonetta*, and three bomb vessels at his disposal, and decided to land an assault force of 3,963 soldiers in two waves. Each wave would consist of two parallel lines of flat-bottomed boats. The first wave embarked two composite battalions of grenadiers commanded by Colonel Howe in the centre (the first battalion comprising companies from the 4th, 17th, 28th, 35th, 42nd, 60th, and 77th regiments, and the second battalion comprising companies from the 15th, 22nd, 27th, 40th, 43rd, 65th, and 95th regiments), a light infantry contingent of battalion strength commanded by Major Moneypenny on the right, and three battalions (Royals, 35th, and 56th) from the 1st and 3rd Brigades under Brigadier Haviland on the left. The second wave was smaller, consisting of a battalion from the 60th Royal Americans also from the 1st Brigade, and a third composite battalion of grenadiers (companies from the 9th, 34th, 56th, and 72nd regiments) commanded by Colonel Carleton. Hervey in the *Dragon*, with *Temeraire* and *Orford*, took position ahead of them and two more ships of the line were stationed on each flank. Farther west at Chorera, Pocock made the appearance of making a landing by having frigates take soundings of the bay and by loading marines into boats.

Before dawn on 7 June, the men congregated on deck for an inspection to ensure they had 40 rounds, two spare flints, and a cloth or leather cover to keep the musket lock dry. At 6.00am the soldiers began to embark. Unfavourable winds and currents caused delay in forming two lines, but Hervey took care to keep each unit 'as connected as possible'. Not until 9.00am was the order to row to shore given. Meanwhile the *Richmond* and *Trent* fired their guns at the landing beach and the woods behind to deter any defenders.

At 10.30am soldiers of the first wave jumped into moderate surf from boats made steady by the bowmen, and waded ashore with loaded muskets high above their heads and their cartridge belts slung over their shoulders. The crews, their boats having been made ready to make a quick exit from the beach by throwing a kedge anchor astern, waited to make a return journey to those transports that flew a navy jack or ensign indicating men were still to go ashore. The soldiers formed up into their parent units facing inland.

Opposition had so far been intermittent. Robertson told how on the left flank at the entrance to the Bacuranao River 'a few guns fired from a small redoubt'. The Spanish occupied 'a small breastwork thrown up by an old tower, but were soon dispersed by the fire from the *Mercury* and *Bonetta*'[1] – a frigate and sloop that were ordered by Keppel to anchor close inshore to silence the battery before it could significantly annoy the landing.

By midday both waves of the assault force had disembarked and the light infantry, accompanied by Albemarle who had landed in the *Valiant*'s barge, began to march along the beach towards the Cojimar River. The river was defended by 'an old, square stone fortress, with about ten guns' as well as 'a breastwork lined with some pieces of cannon and where appeared about 600 men in arms to defend it' (Journal). 'Not finding a good road without first taking possession of the redoubt' Albemarle called for naval support, and Keppel reported to Pocock how he 'sent orders to Captain Hervey to proceed

**JUNE 7
1762**

**Assault waves
land**

With the transports anchored a little off shore, the flat-bottomed boats can be seen landing the soldiers in this Orsbridge print. Farther up the shore the *Dragon* and bomb vessels are bombarding Cojimar Castle. (Lieutenant Orsbridge of the *Orford* made twelve drawings and used the engravers Carnot and Mason to produce prints, which were sold as a full set in 1765). (Anne SK Brown collection)

1 Anon., *An Authentic Journal of the Siege of Havana by an Officer*, London (1762), hereafter referred to as (Journal)

The first wave comprised 49 boats and the second 27 boats. The approach to the beach was carried out 'with great regularity, and without any loss' (Journal). On each boat the two bowmen guided their craft through the shoals. Both Elliot and William Keppel took their place in the boats. (National Army Museum)

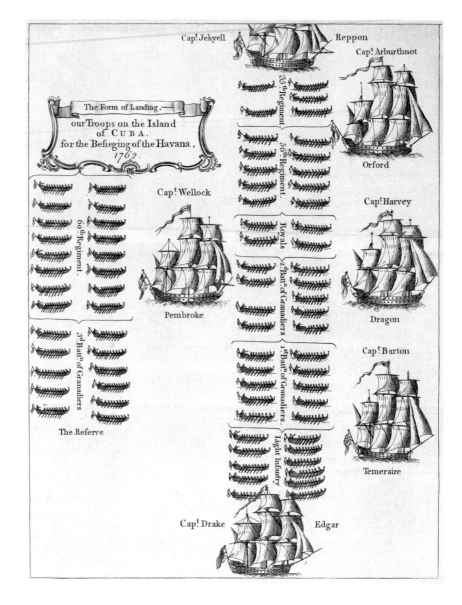

The Form of Landing, our Troops on the Island of CUBA. for the Besieging of the Havana, 1762.

Cap.t Jekyell

Reppon

Cap.t Arburthnot

35th Regiment.

56th Regiment.

Orford

Cap.t Wellock

Royals

Cap.t Harvey

Pembroke

2d Batt.n of Granadiers.

1st Batt.n of Granadiers.

Dragon

60th Regiment.

Cap.t Barton

3d Batt.n of Granadiers

Light Infantry

Temeraire

The Reserve

Cap.t Drake

Edgar

in with the *Dragon* along with the *Bonetta* sloop and *Basilisk* and *Thunder* bombs [ketches] and anchor before it and endeavour to drive the enemy from it'. At 2.30pm a constant bombardment by these ships started, and within the hour the defenders took refuge in the woods after having spiked their guns. At 4.00pm Hervey landed his marines to take possession of the fort, and the light infantry and grenadiers were able to cross the river unmolested.

Guns, horses, ammunition, and other supplies were being disembarked back at the landing beach, as well as the other brigades under General Lafausille. As the sun went down, elements of the landing force were within 2½ miles of El Morro, but had an uncomfortable time 'laying upon their arms that night, with very heavy rains' (Journal). Thunder and lightning greeted the arrival of the British, and the troops became soaked to the skin when the downpour extinguished their fires.

The march inland

The next morning on 8 June, Albemarle led a march inland through the woods to the open country around Guanabacoa. Knowles had recommended an immediate occupation of the heights of La Cabaña, which he had reported 'dominated the Morro, as well as the city'. According to Mackellar, the move inland was justified 'to secure the avenues on that side, and a large tract of country which could supply the army with water, cattle and vegetables', but Knowles would come to criticize this manoeuvre as 'permanently dividing the army'. Carleton, already positioned on the west side of Cojimar stream, proceeded to Guanabacoa with the battalion of light infantry and some grenadiers. Not all the troops were ordered there, however. Howe was told to continue with two grenadier battalions through the Cojimar wood up the slope to El Morro, and by the evening would begin to probe La Cabaña ridge.

At Guanabacoa, Albemarle ran into more opposition than he expected. At 2.00pm he came across a Spanish force deployed on rising ground near the village that included 300 horse from the Edinburgh dragoons and several companies of infantry with a larger force of militia. Robertson described how the cavalry threatened to charge into the British line when they 'marched up in very good order at a slow gallop but retreated upon our people giving them a fire'. The British line then advanced 'and met with a small river which two field pieces with difficulty passed' and formed on rising ground on the other side of the stream. Continuing to move 'briskly towards the enemy', when the Spanish line was 300yds away the two field pieces fired two to three times, which prompted the enemy 'to run off precipitously only firing 2 or 3 straggling shot'. Carleton took the town and at 3.00pm, when Albemarle with the rest of the army arrived, was ordered to proceed back to El Morro. Elliot was left in charge of seven battalions that remained at Guanabacoa, including a detachment under Captain Suttie of the 9th Foot that was mounted on 100 captured horses to round up cattle and act as scouts.

Around Cojimar Fort the first real resistance was encountered (although from Mackellar's description most of the defenders were probably militia rather than regular troops). Naval bombardment cleared the way and the soldiers occupied the fort, with Albemarle establishing his headquarters there that night.

THE LANDING AND APPROACH

7–12 JUNE 1762

After arriving east of Havana on 6 June Pocock orders Keppel to organize a landing and takes twelve ships of the line and the store ships to the west of the city to conduct a feint. On 7 June at 6.00am troops are transferred to longboats but not until 9.30am are they ready to row towards shore.

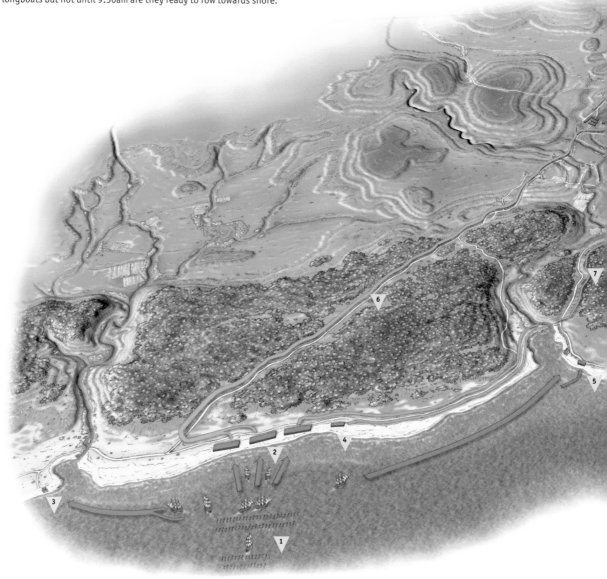

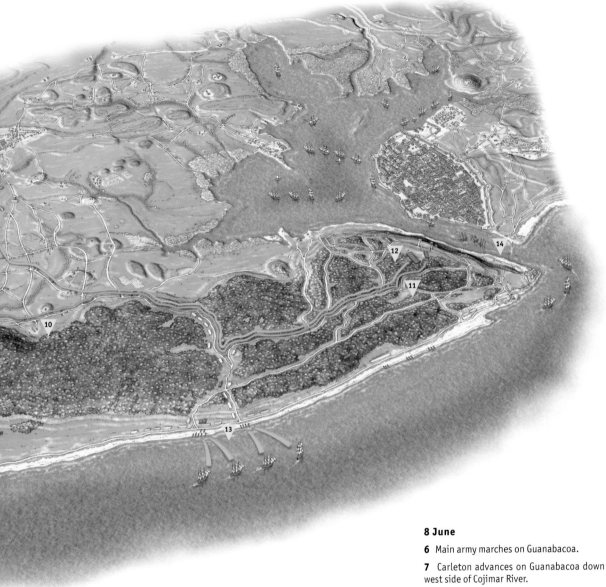

▼ EVENTS

7 June

1 Flat bottomed boats, escorted by six ships of the line and smaller craft, have formed into two waves.

2 *Richmond* and *Trent* fire at the landing beach and the boats hit the beaches at 10.30 am.

3 *Mercury* and *Bonetta* silence the fort at Bacuranao.

4 The Light Infantry battalion forms up and advances on Cojimar castle.

5 *Dragon* and *Bonetta* commence firing at Cojimar castle at 2.30pm and marines are landed at 4.00pm.

8 June

6 Main army marches on Guanabacoa.

7 Carleton advances on Guanabacoa down west side of Cojimar River.

8 Carleton's Light Infantry repels Spanish cavalry charge.

9 Elliot occupies Guanabacoa.

10 Howe's grenadiers move onto the Cabanas.

9–12 June

11 Howe's probe against the Spanish Redoubt prompts the guns to be spiked.

12 Carleton moves onto the Cabanas and assaults Spanish Redoubt on 11 June.

13 Cannon are landed and a siege camp is formed.

14 Spanish sink three ships of the line in the harbour entrance and establish a boom.

KEY

Movements of 7 June

Movements of 8 June

Movements of 9–12 June

The approach to El Morro

Carleton's march from Guanabacoa was a slow, hard slog. Albemarle, who had returned to Cojimar, wrote to Pocock that 'we shall find great difficulty in getting through the wood; it is surprisingly thick'. The approach was up wooded slopes with few proper tracks and contained prickly cacti called 'Spanish bayonet'. Only by the evening of 10 June was Carleton able to position his force for an assault on La Cabaña. Meanwhile the main body was sent back to Cojimar to approach El Morro from that direction.

Luckily Howe's earlier advance on La Cabaña on the night of 8 June had some success. Spanish sailors had managed to drag up seven 18- and 24-pdr guns from the warships, but during the night they were alarmed by probes from Howe's grenadiers; thinking their position about to be stormed, they either spiked their guns or threw them into the harbour, and left the heights to be defended by a small force of militia. The delay imposed upon Carleton by the terrain would therefore not be significant. At 2.00pm on 11 June his light infantry stormed the gun platform, which the British named the 'Spanish Redoubt', chasing the defenders down to boats in the harbour. The two companies he left to occupy the position were quickly targeted from El Morro, batteries in the city, and even shipping in the harbour. One shot killed 14 grenadiers standing in support of the light infantry. The next day work began on a howitzer battery Robertson described as 'to the left of the redoubt to annoy the shipping'. Meanwhile, on the west side of the harbour, a diversion ordered by Pocock ended up occupying Chorera Castle.

On 13 June, with La Cabaña occupied, work could start on the 'Grand Battery', laid down in woods less than 200yds from the walls of El Morro. Dragging the guns inland from the beach through the summer heat required the construction of roads surfaced with heavy logs. Material to construct entrenchments had to be landed near Cojimar and hand-carried to the front line as there were few horses in the tropics. The navy was immediately generous with its manpower; on 9 June Keppel ordered 210 sailors from six ships of the line to land for three days 'to be employed

On 11 June at 4.00am, Chorera Castle was bombarded by the *Belle Isle*, *Bonetta* sloop and *Lurcher* cutter, and at noon marines were landed to occupy the fort, which had been evacuated. Pocock intended the attack as a diversion from the assault on La Cabaña carried out that evening.

under the command of Captain Barton in cutting a road through the woods for drawing the cannon to the army'. The next day he directed Captain McKenzie to gather 300 marines from seven ships and take them to Cojimar to help scour the country for supplies.

Mackellar had been right to warn about the lack of soil and water on the east side. Mante, mentioned as an assistant engineer at Havana, and historian of expeditions in the Americas, described 'the country hereabouts being little better than bare rock and the soil, where any was to be found, exceedingly thin'. Sandbags had to be filled on the beach and then carried 2 miles to the forward positions. Water casks had to be landed from the ships and similarly transported. Keppel wanted a double ration of rum to appease his men, but Pocock refused because a resupply convoy had not arrived from Jamaica and stocks were short. Despite these problems the construction of the Grand Battery began in earnest.

Mante was an engineer by profession, which would explain the detail of the map in his book; in this section the advance inland to Guanabacoa and the siege operations around El Morro are shown. (British Library)

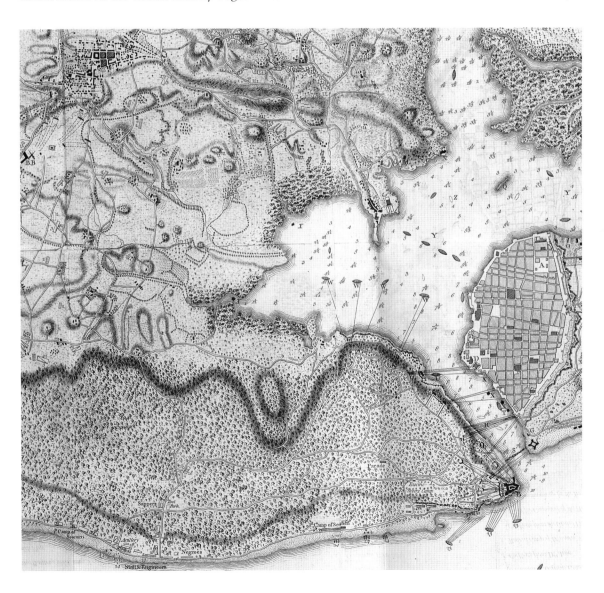

THE SIEGE OF EL MORRO

The construction of the siege works

Artillery and stores were landed between El Morro and Cojimar, making carriage by hand to the siege camp easier. The ability of the navy to rapidly transfer stores, ammunition, and equipment from the ships to the siege camp, unhindered by the enemy, was integral to the successful outcome of amphibious operations in this period. Serres painted all twelve Orsbridge drawings. (National Maritime Museum)

Major General Keppel was in charge of the operations against El Morro. His approach was to build sufficient batteries to knock out the fort's guns and batter a breach in its walls to threaten and, if necessary, carry out an assault. He realized any delays to the siege works could be devastating because of the threat of disease, but the tasks required of his men soon began to mount: constructing batteries and approaches, securing water and food supplies, guarding against sallies from El Morro, and protecting the British camp from an attack from the interior. Yet an early assault of the fort, even if contemplated, would have ended in disaster owing to the ditch that, unknowingly to Keppel, lay before El Morro's landward wall.

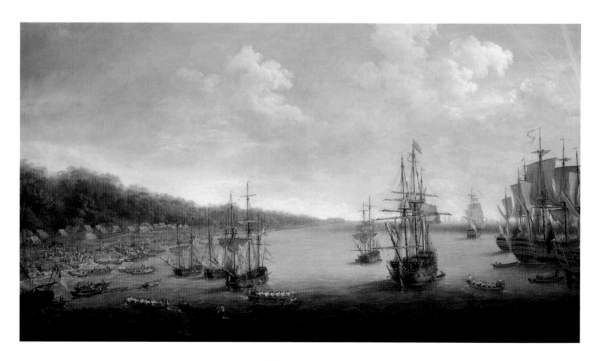

Velasco's strategy was to drag out the siege until the effects of tropical disease took hold of the besiegers. The Grand Battery had been placed out of the line of sight of his guns but he 'opened up some more embrasures on one of the bastions of the Morro, from which they fired grapeshot, and much annoyed our people in the wood' (Journal). Intermittent and indiscriminate fire was also given from Spanish warships in the harbour. Another threat came from Cuban irregulars operating in the woods, preying on those foraging for supplies. Commodore Keppel wrote in his journal how 'some stragglers of the enemy's dragoons and mounted peasantry lurked about the woods and took several seamen belonging to our transports'. Seamen were particularly prone to roam, and in one incident 'a party of sailors belonging to an English frigate going on shore at the Havannah in search of fresh provisions were surrounded by the enemy and thirteen of them cut to pieces in a very inhuman manner'. On another occasion Captain Walker of the *Lurcher* was killed whilst exploring upriver.

Commodore Keppel specifically mentioned to Pocock atrocities that had been committed on 70 British seamen. Pocock complained to Prado alleging 'several seamen belonging to His Britannic Majesty's fleet under my command have been barbarously treated when taken prisoner by the Spaniards'. He trusted that Prado was 'agreeable to the principles of humanity' and 'that we shall never deviate from the constant practice of civilized countries'. This letter was never delivered; Prado refused to receive the envoys trusted with its carriage, Colonel Carleton and Captain Elphinston.

The weather was unpredictable. At first 'operations were much retarded by the continual rains' (Journal). However, from 21 June a drought set in and the sun blazed down incessantly for the next 14 days. The lack of water threatened to debilitate the army and was most severely felt by the labourers

JUNE 11 1762

La Cabaña captured

Hervey reported to Keppel how Spanish fire had left 'my masts and rigging much cut about, and only one anchor'. Damage was severe (losses had been worst on the *Cambridge*, with 24 killed and 95 wounded) but not as bad as in this Spanish depiction. (Bridgeman Art)

at the siege works. Albemarle wrote to Pocock that he was so distressed for water with this dry weather that 'unless you are so good to assist us, I don't know what we shall do'. On 15 June, in order to secure a water supply and also cut off the streams that supplied Havana, Howe landed at Chorera with two battalions of grenadiers, 300 light infantry, and 800 marines. Water had to be transported from there to the landing beach near Cojimar and then manhandled to the men working on the batteries. Even so, Mante recorded how 'so scanty and precarious was this supply that they were obliged to have recourse to water from the ships'. Commodore Keppel wrote in his diary 'their want of that article is frequently so pressing that we are obliged to land water from the ships'. Despite these measures, Private Miller told how 'a dollar was frequently given for a pint of water', which could still be tainted and cause dysentery. Within hours of the Grand Battery opening, lack of water would threaten to ruin the whole expedition.

Besides the Grand Battery other batteries were prepared. On 22 June 'a bomb battery down by the seaside was opened ... with great success, having 3 mortars and 20 royals' (Journal). The intention of this battery was 'to draw the enemy's fire from the workers at the battery'. On La Cabaña, the howitzers began firing on 24 June 'against the ships in the harbour, which obliged them to remove next day'. Another battery of two 13in howitzers was started on the 'White Road', to the left of the howitzers near the Spanish Redoubt, to fire on shipping in the harbour and also the town. Next to the Grand Battery, Keppel agreed to construct a battery of four guns. On 22 June Captain Williams marked this out to the left and rear of the Grand Battery, 464yds from El Morro and behind a parallel on which work had begun the previous day for a line of marksmen. Another parallel for mortars was started to the left of the Grand Battery on 25 June, under the direction of Captain Dixon, 233yds from El Morro. However, building the wooden

Although the naval bombardment did not have the intended effect, Mackellar reported the ships 'still did us a considerable service in taking up the enemy's attention for that time which gained us a superiority in the number of guns'. (National Maritime Museum)

platforms for the batteries, making several thousand sandbags and hundreds of mantelets for their protection, and bringing up enough ammunition for a sustained barrage served to delay the reduction of El Morro.

Crucially, Pocock had trust in the judgement of his army colleagues and was willing to assist them, requesting Commodore Keppel to 'supply the army with guns, ammunition, and men as far as he finds proper'. Sailors were resourceful and the fleet 'supplied us with old sails and biscuit bags which they make into bags for us. Several hundred square pieces of old junk and cordage were made by them to serve as mantelets' (Journal). As soon as 25 June Albemarle acknowledged the navy's role, and he wrote to Pocock, 'we must have given up our undertaking long ago without the ample assistance we receive from you and the Commodore'.

Pocock's willingness to provide men to work ashore was admirable because sailors were a finite resource. Without them a ship of the line was vulnerable, especially in the hurricane season. Commodore Keppel wrote 'the fate of the fleet if a hurricane catches us is not pleasant reflecting upon'. At least a safe, alternative anchorage for the transports was provided when the *Defiance* and *Hampton Court*, cruising west of Havana, took the Spanish frigates *Venganza* and *Marte* at anchor in Mariel Harbour, west of Chorera.

The first Spanish sortie

The progress of the works had not gone unnoticed by Velasco. He persuaded Prado to sanction an assault on the siege works during the pre-dawn hours of 29 June, but there is debate about how many troops came from the town and how many from El Morro. One account contends the Spanish 'threw over in boats about 600 men from the Havana with intent to surprise and burn our batteries' with approximately another 500 men coming from El Morro (Journal). Robertson noted that a total of 1,000 men were involved, including 500 grenadiers that had embarked from Havana at 2.00am. The historian David Syrett stated that 260 Spanish regulars and seamen came from Havana and 506 regulars and marines from El Morro. Whatever the true figure, when the Spanish landed between El Morro and the Spanish Redoubt at 4.00am the threat to the British positions was very real. Robertson reported:

> Part of the grenadiers pushed through the wood, passed by the 4 gun battery [Williams'] without observing it and formed at the crossroads where the guns for the 10 gun battery were standing, where they were attacked by a *picquet* of ours consisting of a captain and 60 men, and routed, with the loss of about 20 men killed and wounded. Our losses did not exceed 10 killed and wounded. The number of that body of Spanish was about 200.

Another group attacked the parallel to the left of the Grand Battery (Dixon's), passed it, and then came into the rear, but was repulsed. The third force threatened the howitzer battery near the Spanish Redoubt, but was 'drove off by a much inferior force with the loss of about 30 men killed and wounded'. As dawn broke, 200 Spanish were either dead or made prisoner, many having been

THE SIEGE AND CAPTURE OF EL MORRO

13 JUNE–31 JULY 1762

The building of gun batteries to dismantle El Morro's guns and make siege approaches possible commences on 13 June. Because soil is scarce on the rocky headland trenches cannot be dug; instead sandbags have to be filled on the beach and along with other siege materials carried forward to the battery sites.

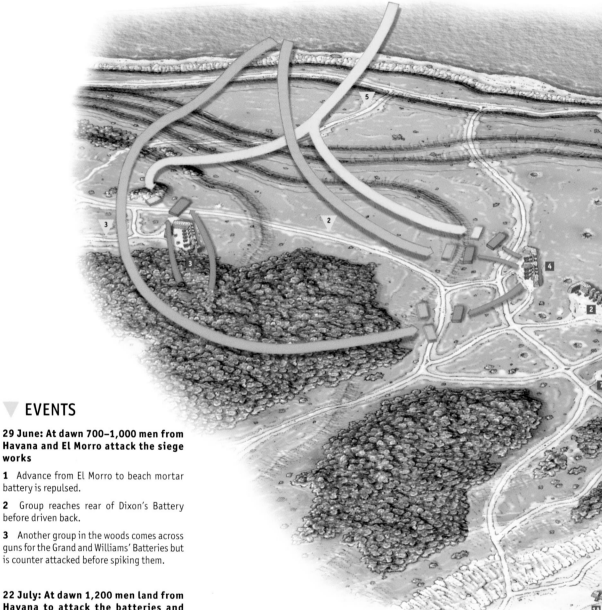

▼ EVENTS

29 June: At dawn 700–1,000 men from Havana and El Morro attack the siege works

1 Advance from El Morro to beach mortar battery is repulsed.

2 Group reaches rear of Dixon's Battery before driven back.

3 Another group in the woods comes across guns for the Grand and Williams' Batteries but is counter attacked before spiking them.

22 July: At dawn 1,200 men land from Havana to attack the batteries and miners

4 Advance from beach fails to reach saps and miners.

5 Attempt on Williams' and Dixon's Batteries counter attacked by 60th Royal Americans

29 July: During the night Spanish naval attack on miners

6 Spanish craft attack the miners with grapeshot but are repelled by the guard force.

LOCATIONS ①-③

1 Positions of British ships for naval bombardment, 1 July

2 Saps laid to El Morro, 17–20 July.

3 Location of mines laid in counterscarp and seaward bastion, 20–30 July.

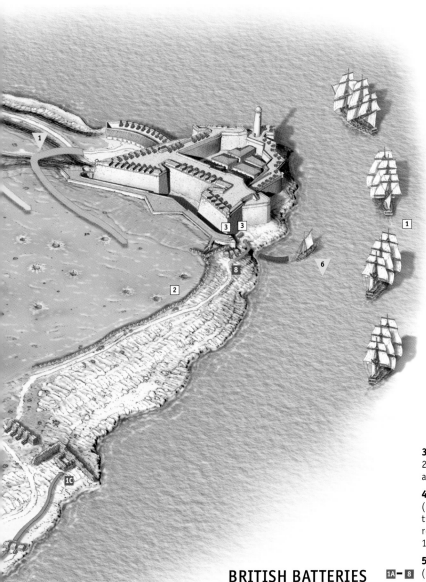

BRITISH BATTERIES 1A-8

1A Beach Mortar (500) – Opens 24 June (two 13in mortars, one 10in mortar, fourteen 5in mortars). Moves forward to **1B**. and then to the Stone Redoubt at **1C** (320).

2 Grand (192) – Opens 1 July (eight 24-pdrs and two 15in mortars). Destroyed by fire 2–11 July and converted into musket line.

3 Williams' (464) – Opens 1 July (four 24-pdrs and two 13in mortars). Three 24-pdrs are added on 9 July.

4 Dixon's (233) – Opens 1 July (originally with two 10in mortars and twelve 5in mortars), converted and reopens 9 July (five 24-pdrs and two 10in mortars).

5 Fuzer's (320) – Opens 11 July (originally 12-pdrs, destroyed by gunfire on 13 July and 24-pdrs probably installed)

6 Durnford's (290) – Opens 13 July (four 32-pdrs)

7 Valiant's (290) – Opens 17 July (four 32-pdrs)

8 One 24-pdr, one 12-pdr and eighteen coehorns moved up to glacis.

wounded. Several Spanish soldiers 'lay in the bushes all day, some prisoners being taken in the afternoon by accidentally falling on them in the bushes'.

The British had benefited from the woods protecting the whereabouts of the batteries. Robertson concluded that the timing of the Spanish assault could not have been better as 'next day our two gun batteries were to be finished, and the guns for them were on the road where the enemy were first stopped by our *picquet*, so that had they had spirit to have pushed on they might have spiked them all up'. However, this may have been more coincidence than design. Robertson suggested that their focus was on the mortars near the beach and the guns on the Spanish Redoubt and that they were 'quite ignorant of our batteries being so far advanced'. The Grand Battery was completed later that afternoon. The bombardment would start next morning; concurrently Captain Hervey would lead an attack by four ships of the line on the seaward side. Albemarle expected the land batteries would open a breach for an assault party that day.

The bombardment

The plan for the naval attack was for the *Stirling Castle* to sail along the north side of El Morro to 'cover the anchoring' of the *Dragon*, *Marlborough*, and *Cambridge*. Pocock and Keppel both had misgivings about the operation, which were soon realized. The ships caught a breeze at 7.00am, but the *Stirling Castle*, supposed to be leading, soon fell behind. Hervey sent an officer to enquire why and was told by Captain Campbell that most of the ship's sails, yards and booms had been taken down to protect them from damage, even though Hervey could clearly see the main- and spritsails 'in place, but furled'. Hervey's force was one ship down before the attack began. The remaining three ships pushed on.

The *Cambridge* was the first ship to anchor beneath El Morro's walls, just after 9.00am, followed a little later by the *Dragon* and then the *Marlborough*. A heavy exchange of fire created such a billowing smoke that neither side could see the fall of shot. However, it became obvious that the guns on the ships could not be sufficiently elevated to hit El Morro's embrasures. The Spanish could not depress their guns sufficiently to target the ships' hulls either, but were able to significantly damage the masts and rigging.

Hervey persisted in his bombardment, describing how the smoke made it impossible to 'tell when the army will advance', but as the tide fell the *Dragon* went aground. Hervey sent a note to Keppel requesting direction and explained:

> I am unluckily aground but my guns bear. I cannot perceive their fire to slacken… I am afraid they are too high to do the execution we wished. I have many men out of combat now, and officers wounded.

In order to be refloated, he asked Keppel for a 'frigate to drop a bower [anchor] off, and send the end of the cable on board here'. In the event no frigate was sent. Hervey then ordered Captain Campbell to send a cable attached to one of *Stirling Castle*'s anchors but Campbell refused. The battering of the *Dragon* continued, with other ships of the squadron also receiving a hard pounding.

Eventually, at 2.00pm Keppel sent an order to disengage. Hervey had to try and heave himself off. Stores were loaded into boats and hoisted overboard, and water barrels were broken up to lighten the ship. One of the ship's boats took the last anchor out and a heave on the capstan finally wrenched the ship free. The *Dragon* withdrew accompanied by the rest of the squadron. A total of 192 officers and men had been killed or wounded.

Little damage had been done to El Morro's walls, but by targeting the ships the Spanish defenders had neglected the landward side. Fire from the Grand Battery 'was poured in with redoubled fury'. However, according to Mackellar, 'the moment the Spaniards were free from the fire of our ships, they again returned to the front our batteries played on, and returned our fire with much briskness'. No breach was made, despite Albemarle's predictions. The Spanish were exhausted, but that night 554 men were sent across the harbour to relieve the garrison, taking with them more ammunition and replacement gun carriages.

The next day the land batteries fired with great success, the Spanish seldom firing back (the opening two days of bombardment caused them 40 dead and 196 wounded) but then calamity struck: 'Unhappily, about noon, we were obliged to slacken, the battery being in danger of catching fire, from the constant fire kept up, and the dryness of the fascines.' The embers caught and at first the crew and guards laboured successfully to extinguish them, but at 2.00am the next day more flames took hold 'with great violence'. Mackellar called this 'a mortifying stroke' and wrote 'thus was the labour of seventeen days, of five or six hundred men, destroyed in a few hours'. Attempts to extinguish the fires and repair some embrasures were made during the next few nights but 'the enemy's fire obliged the men to give them up'.

The battle of the batteries

Mackellar believed locating the battery so close to El Morro was a mistake that 'protracted the siege at least three weeks longer than it otherwise would have been'. More batteries would have to be constructed 'placed at double the distance from the Morro'. A quick win was had when Dixon's mortar battery in the left parallel was converted into one for cannon, and Williams' Battery was expanded by adding two more embrasures. On 11 July a new four-gun battery left of the Stone Redoubt and 320yds from El Morro (called Fuzer's Battery), together with two guns in the saved portion of the Grand Battery, opened fire; adding the seven guns in Williams' and five in Dixon's, a total of 18 guns, besides mortars, were available.

The battle of the batteries continued. The British found it difficult to permanently suppress the Spanish guns in El Morro. Hundreds of rounds were fired every day, knocking masonry from the walls and causing splinters to fly into the interior, but the Spanish returned fire with eight or nine guns and were 'very brisk in remounting their cannon' (Journal). Mackellar noted that before noon on 11 July, because of constant use 'two guns in the left parallel failed, one by running, the other by cracking; the carriage of a third was disabled on Williams' battery'. In the afternoon, 'the merlons of the Grand Battery again caught fire' and this time 'the whole was irreparably consumed', but at least the

This picture of the Grand Battery is too stylized to be accurate, with an outwardly calm and ordered appearance. In Mackellar's opinion the protection afforded to the batteries was superior to El Morro's thin layer of masonry, but the dryness of the fascines and lack of water would undo all the effort expended on this fortification. (National Maritime Museum)

JUNE 13
1762

Work on the
Grand Battery
begins

disabled guns in the other batteries were replaced during the night and in total 16 guns were ready to fire at daybreak. Nevertheless, losses were continuous, and on 12 July the carriages of three guns in the Stone Redoubt were disabled. The Spanish were also replacing damaged guns during the night and every four to six days the garrison was replaced with a fresh one from the city.

On 13 July the opening of the first 32-pdr battery proved to be a turning point. Crewed by the navy, commanded by Captain Lindsay, and named 'Durnford' after the engineer that constructed it, the battery was located on the right parallel 290yds from the seaward bastion. Not only did it show the commitment of the navy to the siege works (for example on 8 July Keppel described in his journal how 'the Admiral sent up 300 seamen with officers to strengthen the sea detachments, which have casualties of upward of 800 men'), but the added firepower over the coming days meant a 'more constant and heavy fire was kept on the castle than ever before' (Journal). Mackellar recounted how this battery caused 'considerable havoc' on its first day, so much so that 'another 32 pdr battery was ordered to be made upon the right of it'. By 14 July 'there were twenty guns against five or six of the enemy's … before dark they were reduced to two' and on the next day 'the enemy's fire was totally silenced before night'. On 17 July the second naval battery of four 32-pdrs named the 'Valiant' was opened, again 290yds from El Morro.

The persistent firing of all these guns placed a huge demand on supplies of shot and powder. On 11 July, 450 shot (32lb) and 900 wads, as well as 1,500 wads for 24lb shot, were unloaded. Keppel wrote how three ships of the line had given up all their stocks. By mid-July up to 1,000 shot were required daily, and on 17 July Keppel told Pocock supplies were falling dangerously low. On 15 July Albemarle wrote to the Governor of Jamaica requesting 1,000 barrels of gunpowder as well as shot, and Pocock sent a ship of the line to transport them. Prado recorded in his diary that, in total, 18,104 rounds fell on El Morro and 3,070 on La Punta.

The siege approaches to the ditch

Now that a superiority of fire had been achieved, approaches to the walls could be started; because of the rocky nature of the land these had to be above ground rather than dug as trenches. The aim was to cross the glacis (the natural slope in front of the fort that was arranged to be swept by musket or cannon fire) to reach the seaward bastion. Here in front of the covered way was a levelled surface for a small battery, too vulnerable for the Spanish to be able to hold but potentially extremely useful to the besiegers. Gabions (wickerwork cylinders filled with earth) stuffed with fascines (long bundles of bound sticks) were used in order to advance the sap. From 8 July each soldier had been ordered to make two fascines when off duty and 'the 40th Regiment was employed in making gabions; the men of war in making junk, blinds, or mantelet' (Journal).

On 17 July work on the sap began but 'there being a thick thorny wood to cut through was advanced but little way'. In total, 315yds separated the British lines from the ditch and this had to be covered by a line of barricades. Two or three Spanish guns had managed to fire but each time had been soon

On 17 July Pocock had this map of the batteries made for a report to Anson. The Grand Battery's advanced location (point D) is clearly apparent. From mid-July, El Morro suffered around 500 direct hits and 30 casualties each day. Anson would never see the map as he died on 7 June. (Staffordshire Record Office)

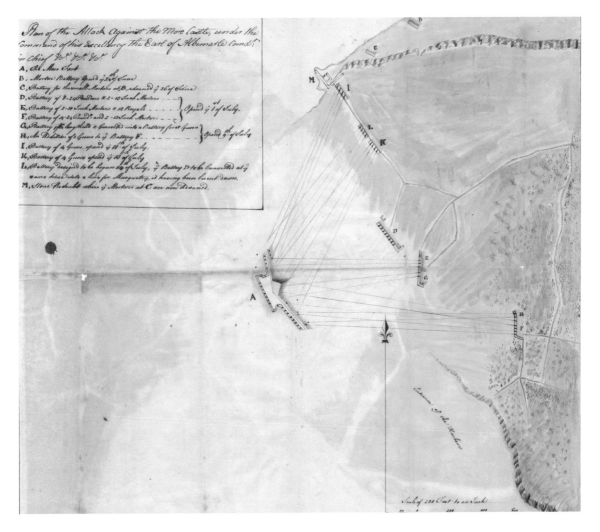

silenced; however, the risk of musketry and wall pieces still made advancing the sap a hazardous occupation. The next night was different, with two-thirds of the distance achieved. By noon on 19 July the covered way before the seaward bastion was reached, and that evening work began on a sap along the feature. A lodgement was made for a line of musketry to target the top of the fortress walls to drive off enemy gunners.

The existence of the ditch had first been established on 12 July but now its immense depth was fully appreciated. Carleton inspected the obstacle at first hand and reported 'the ditch extremely deep but narrow'. When Commodore Douglas arrived with the Jamaica convoy, 600 cotton bags were purchased 'which was thought would help to fill in the ditch upon an emergency', but the proper reconnaissance showed that 'the thoughts of filling it … were found impracticable' (Journal).

The only way of dealing with the obstruction was to attempt to blow both the bastion and counterscarp into the ditch to fill the void with debris, which an assaulting party could scramble over. A call for miners was served throughout the fleet. Keppel asked for 40, but in total 60–70 men were found. The counterscarp was easily accessed from the sap; the bastion, however, was another matter. Fortunately there was 'a thin edge of rock left at the point of the bastion, to cover the extremity of the ditch from being open to the sea'. Mackellar recounted how on the morning of 20 July, along this ridge 'the miner passed with some difficulty to the foot of the wall, which he could do nowhere else without the help of scaling ladders'. The miners had to take their chance crossing this feature and surprisingly 'it cost only three or four men during the whole time'. Additional work to dig a shaft for sinking explosives into the counterscarp was started but delayed by large stones.

On 20 July six coehorns (small portable mortars set in wooden blocks) were brought up from the Stone Redoubt to the site of the small battery in front of the covered way; one 12-pdr and one 24-pdr were also dragged there. The following day 12 more coehorns were brought up. Such was the ability of the British to bring fire to bear upon the walls, the Spanish defenders were forced to keep their heads down; so much so that during the night a sergeant and a party of 12 men were able to scale the wall a little to the right of the mine and 'found about nine or ten men asleep in that part of the work'. The Spaniards awoke before the men could reach them and raised the alarm. Mackellar optimistically thought that 'had it been possible to have succoured this party briskly, the fort might have been carried'. Both sides had been given an indication of what was to come and Velasco, unable to re-establish a gun line on the battlements, was intent on launching a large sortie to dislodge the miners and delay an assault – perhaps decisively, as yellow fever had taken hold in the British camp and there were no signs of the arrival of the American reinforcements that were now more urgently required than ever.

THE ASSAULT OF EL MORRO

The second Spanish sortie

On 21 July, when the British were beginning to suffer badly from disease and still had no prospect of reinforcement, Prado flung 1,200 Spanish regulars, seamen, and militia across the harbour to attempt to set the fascine batteries and saps on fire. As dawn broke the Spanish began to push up the bank. The first party got behind one of the batteries but was stopped by a guard of 30 men under Lieutenant Colonel Stuart of the 90th Foot, long enough for the third battalion of the 60th Royal Americans to come to their aid. Robertson described how the 'enemy were then driven down the hill with great slaughter'. As many men took to boats as could, others attempted to swim and 'there were one hundred and fifty of them drowned'. The second party tried to attack the sappers on the glacis but musket fire from the sap along the covered way beat them off. The third party went up to the Spanish Redoubt 'but finding the guard there reinforced, and ready to receive them, they returned very peaceably from where they came'. One account described how 'these poor wretches, militia natives, mulattoes, negroes, and some seamen, left about 400 dead upon the spot, many wounded, and about 70 prisoners' (Journal). This was perhaps an excessive figure as Prado admitted to only 32 killed and 'an infinite number wounded'. The British loss was 'only fifty men killed and wounded'. Carleton was amongst them, receiving 'a small shot in the arm, which broke the bone'. Mackellar admitted that if this attack had been successful, it would have been 'impossible for the exhausted troops to have collected materials to form the siege anew'.

The attack had been a desperate failure and its repulse must have been a relief to the British, but the work on the mines – slow, dangerous, and arduous – pressed on. The batteries continued to give covering fire, some of which bore fruit. Mackellar told how on 26 July a 'merchant-frigate of two decks [the *Perla*], which had annoyed the British, was sunk by a howitzer from Dixon's battery'. On 28 July another 'large merchant ship of the enemy's caught fire by

JUNE 29
1762

**The first
Spanish sortie**

lightning, within the harbour, and blew up in about ten minutes'. The next day Albemarle tried to scare the defenders into leaving El Morro, ordering 'cannon to be fired without shot'. He hoped 'we shall learn the enemy's base of fire and disposition of their troops against the mine', and optimistically thought 'if a panic should take them we may profit from it'. No panic occurred, but that night one further Spanish attempt to delay the miners was launched as two Spanish schooners and a floating battery sent out of the harbour fired grape and small arms; however, 'the covering party fired so smartly upon them, that they were obliged to retire'. Albemarle tried to persuade Velasco to surrender, writing that the King of Spain 'would be the first to order you to capitulate … to preserve such an illustrious and distinguished an officer'. Velasco defiantly replied that his troops 'shall intimate the constancy of their captain' and 'there is still much to expect of fortune'.

The effects of disease

Despite the repulse of the last Spanish attack, the army was 'now so reduced by sickness, that we had a melancholy prospect' (Journal). The effects of disease were so extensive that Private James Miller 'supposed that we should be obliged to re-embark without taking the place'. The new commander of the artillery, Lieutenant Colonel Cleavland, described the illness: 'Fluxes and intermitting fevers is the general disorder, occasioned chiefly by violent heats and great damps in the night.' In July he reported 5,000 soldiers and 3,000 sailors were laid up with various distempers. Major Moneypenny wrote how Albemarle had to draw in the force at Guanabacoa 'about two miles towards the edge of the wood, where the army lay' because by 15 July, only 400 of the 2,500 men originally stationed were fit for duty.

As early as 2 July Albemarle 'wished the North Americans were come'. On 13 July he reported to Egremont the 'increasing sickness of the troops, the intense heat of the weather, and the approaching rainy season are circumstances which prevent me from being too sanguine as to our future success against the town, particularly as we have no news of the American reinforcements'. In his next report four days later, in more stark terms Albemarle warned, 'if the North Americans do not arrive, and very soon, I shall be at a great loss how to proceed'.

Keppel articulated the same concerns. He wrote in his journal how 'the sickness in the squadrons increases every day, and it is with difficulty we find men for the many services the army require from the ships and at the same time keep the detachments on shore relieved'. He confided the increase of sickness at the Valiant Battery was 'most distressful', and noted men of the naval detachment 'fall down sick very fast'. On 17 July he wrote to Pocock that if the North Americans 'are not here soon, it will indeed be very unfortunate that so much zeal and perseverance, both on your side and Lord Albemarle's, should not succeed for want of numbers'.

JUNE 30
1762

**The bombardment
begins**

The journey of the Americans

The Americans had been delayed because the government's dispatch to General Amherst in New York to send a force of 4,000 men to Havana had been intercepted, and not until 1 April did his instructions arrive. He immediately ordered down the 46th and 58th regiments from Canada and Gorham's Rangers (a 253-strong regular company of North American colonials) from Nova Scotia. Four regular New York independent companies, each of 80 men, were also made ready. However, the main American contingent had to be raised from scratch. Amherst wrote to the colonial governors of New Jersey, Rhode Island, Connecticut, and New York asking them to provide a specified number of provincials for the expedition, but stated the destination must remain a secret; Connecticut was to supply 1,033, Rhode Island 217, New Jersey 222, and New York 533. He emphasized 'the sooner the men are here [New York] the better'. The New

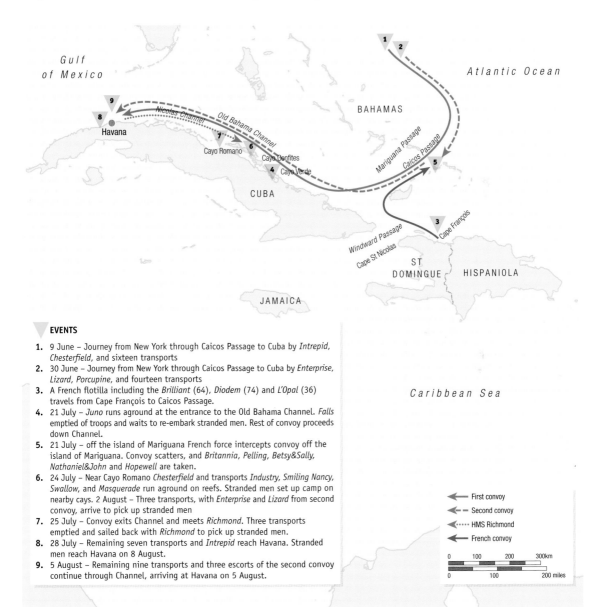

EVENTS

1. 9 June – Journey from New York through Caicos Passage to Cuba by *Intrepid*, *Chesterfield*, and sixteen transports
2. 30 June – Journey from New York through Caicos Passage to Cuba by *Enterprise*, *Lizard*, *Porcupine*, and fourteen transports
3. A French flotilla including the *Brilliant* (64), *Diodem* (74) and *L'Opal* (36) travels from Cape François to Caicos Passage.
4. 21 July – *Juno* runs aground at the entrance to the Old Bahama Channel. *Falls* emptied of troops and waits to re-embark stranded men. Rest of convoy proceeds down Channel.
5. 21 July – off the island of Mariguana French force intercepts convoy off the island of Mariguana. Convoy scatters, and *Britannia*, *Pelling*, *Betsy&Sally*, *Nathaniel&John* and *Hopewell* are taken.
6. 24 July – Near Cayo Romano *Chesterfield* and transports *Industry*, *Smiling Nancy*, *Swallow*, and *Masquerade* run aground on reefs. Stranded men set up camp on nearby cays. 2 August – Three transports, with *Enterprise* and *Lizard* from second convoy, arrive to pick up stranded men
7. 25 July – Convoy exits Channel and meets *Richmond*. Three transports emptied and sailed back with *Richmond* to pick up stranded men.
8. 28 July – Remaining seven transports and *Intrepid* reach Havana. Stranded men reach Havana on 8 August.
9. 5 August – Remaining nine transports and three escorts of the second convoy continue through Channel, arriving at Havana on 5 August.

York assembly believed that once recruited, their men would be forced into regular regiments in the West Indies, an opinion which Amherst's letter served only to strengthen. An extra 40s (£2) above the £10 bounty given to each man had to be voted through to persuade New Yorkers to serve (wages were £2 a month). In comparison, men from Rhode Island under Lieutenant Colonel Hargill received a bounty of £5, though according to Amherst 'there were [among them] a good many boys, hardly able to carry arms'.

In March, before the notification of the expedition arrived, Connecticut had already voted to raise two regiments for military service under Major General Lyman. Lyman warned that the provincials had an 'unconquerable dislike … against any service in the hot climates' but despite his concerns, the 1st Regiment (minus the 10th Company) was earmarked for the Havana expedition; the 2nd Regiment (with this 10th company) would be sent to Canada. Both Roswell Park, a sergeant in Captain Suffield's company who had left a wife and child in Connecticut when he volunteered for this potentially hazardous operation, and Israel Putnam, a company commander, embarked from New London for New York, arriving on 25 May. However, the reluctance of the New Yorkers meant that their contingent would not fully assemble until 12 June. Furthermore, the 58th Foot and Gorham's Rangers would not arrive from Canada until 7 June. Amherst therefore decided to send his troops in two batches.

On 9 June the Connecticut, Rhode Island, and New Jersey units, plus the Independent companies and 46th Regiment, embarked in 16 transports, with Park among them on board the *Falls*. Under the command of Commodore Hale, the convoy sailed down to Sandy Hook escorted by the *Intrepid* and *Chesterfield*. Contrary winds delayed them here for several days and the *Intrepid* temporarily became 'stuck fast aground'. Not before 19 July was Cuba sighted, and that night in a 'strong gale of wind and the sea foaming', the transport *Masquerade* nearly took the *Falls* in its bow. The following day the *Juno* went aground and at midnight all 121 men on board took to rafts. The *Falls* was ordered to remain behind to pick them up and the transport's complement, including Park, were transferred to the *Intrepid*. The rations were much better on the warship. On the transports a ration of one and a half biscuits a day and an allowance of meat for two days that 'could be put into his mouth all at once' meant 'some men said they should starve to death; some talked of jumping overboard, others wished us to be taken'. Park thought the only problem he had on the *Intrepid* was trouble sleeping 'by reason of being flung this way and that'. However, the prospect of a passage through the Bahama Channel still lay ahead.

In a letter to the convoy commanders, Pocock gave them discretion in whether to attempt the Old Bahama Channel, even suggesting an alternative route around the south coast of Cuba; but he advised staying well clear of Santiago de Cuba, where he said two Spanish ships were based. He also mentioned the threat from Blenac's squadron. The *Port Mahon* and *Hampshire*, instructed to cruise off Cape St Nicholas, carried the letters. In expectation that Hale would take the safe route, Pocock also sent a ship to the west end of Cuba with an order for the Commodore to send his fastest

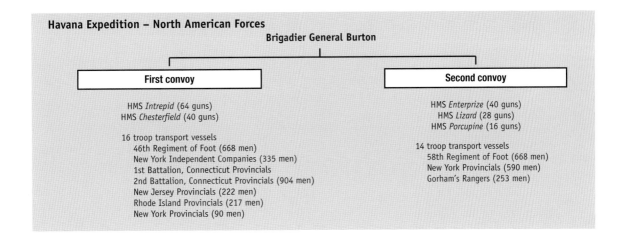

Havana Expedition – North American Forces

Brigadier General Burton

First convoy

HMS *Intrepid* (64 guns)
HMS *Chesterfield* (40 guns)

16 troop transport vessels
46th Regiment of Foot (668 men)
New York Independent Companies (335 men)
1st Battalion, Connecticut Provincials
2nd Battalion, Connecticut Provincials (904 men)
New Jersey Provincials (222 men)
Rhode Island Provincials (217 men)
New York Provincials (90 men)

Second convoy

HMS *Enterprize* (40 guns)
HMS *Lizard* (28 guns)
HMS *Porcupine* (16 guns)

14 troop transport vessels
58th Regiment of Foot (668 men)
New York Provincials (590 men)
Gorham's Rangers (253 men)

transports forward. Much to Pocock's frustration, his instructions never reached their recipients, and when Captain Usher of the *Hampshire* decided to come off station to bring in a prize, Pocock criticized him for having 'shown want of judgement'. In case the convoys still came down the channel, Pocock sent Elphinston in the *Richmond* to escort them, but he failed to reach the east end of the channel before the transports arrived.

On 24 July at daybreak, the *Intrepid* fired 20 warning shots. Looking back Park saw the reason for the emergency signal – four transports and the *Chesterfield* were aground on reefs near Cayo Confites. The sea was beating hard against the stranded ships and some of their masts were broken, but observing the men going ashore on two small nearby cays Hale 'left them to the good hand of providence and stood our course'. When the *Richmond* came across the convoy at the western end of the channel, Elphinston and Hale decided to transfer soldiers from three transports, crowd them onto the others, and then send the emptied ships to pick up the stranded men. Hale continued to Havana, and landed the soldiers from his seven remaining transports on 28 July. The three transports sent back (joined by the *Enterprise* and *Lizard* detached from the second convoy) safely picked up 594 men from the cays on 2 August and arrived at Havana six days later.

The second convoy, commanded by Captain Banks on board the *Lizard*, had not left New York until 30 June because of the difficulty finding transports; 14 were eventually loaded with troops and the convoy then set sail accompanied by the *Porcupine* and *Enterprise*. The passage was similarly fraught, but this time because of enemy action. Captain Corkett had been monitoring Cape François, but on 1 July he had sailed to Havana to report to Pocock. Much to Pocock's disgust, the senior officer at Port Royal failed to maintain a ship watching the port and the French were free to roam. On 21 July, in the Caicos Passage at the southern point of the Bahamas off the island of Mariguana (Mayaguana), the French ships *Diodem* (74), *Brilliant* (64), and *L'Opal* (36), escorting six merchantmen, came across the convoy, which immediately scattered. Five transports were seized, carrying 396 men of the 58th Foot and 92 New York provincials. Major Gorham, who was on the *Delaware* transport 'a common shot to the windward, and a little ahead

For the final assault on El Morro, Keppel made available the *Alcide* (pictured) to deter Spanish boats, and a number of armed boats carrying marines in case of need. (Anne SK Brown collection)

of the enemy with the night to favour us', only narrowly escaped. The remnants of the convoy reunited and reached Havana on 5 August.

Overall, 3,188 men eventually arrived from New York. Though late, Pocock wrote 'they come very seasonably, as sickness amongst the soldiers and seamen increased daily'. Park expected to go ashore on the El Morro side, but instead all the Americans disembarked at Chorera. He marched 1½ miles inland to pitch his tent and walked over a hill to see 'a very grand affair … the city of Havana with all the fine buildings, churches, nunneries, the grand battery, the Governor's fort in town … the finest land I ever saw … coconut trees, cabbage trees, canaries, grapes, cattle, ass, mule'. And from across the bay he heard the incessant sound of a 'grand firing all that night from the batteries'.

The assault across the ditch

On 30 July the mines were at last ready. The initial storming party consisted of three sections of 12 men, each led by a Lieutenant: Charles Forbes, Nugent, and Holyrod. In total, 321 men commanded by Lieutenant Colonel James Stuart of the 90th Foot were listed in the official return for the assault force. The rest of the 1st Brigade, including the 60th Royal Americans, was ready to follow under Keppel. The official Spanish return counted 18 regular army officers, 280 regular soldiers, four marine officers, 200 marines, and 94 armed Negroes. Expecting an assault, Velasco had asked for instructions from Prado but received an ambiguous reply. Velasco hoped the rock would be too solid for the British mines to make an impression.

At 2.00pm the mines were blown. After the smoke cleared, Keppel could see that the explosion in the counterscarp had failed to collapse the outer wall of the ditch, but Mackellar described how the mine in the bastion 'having thrown down a part of both faces made a breach, which the General and chief engineer thought practicable'. Stuart ordered the storming party forward and Forbes, with his men following, rushed over the covered way, safely negotiated the ridge of rock and clambered over the rubble into the

JULY 21 1762

The second Spanish sortie

bastion. The other two groups led by Nugent and Holyrod were close behind, with ladders to assist them where necessary.

Captain Montez, a staff officer at El Morro, told how the mine had blown up 'some of our advanced sentinels … and also some of the seamen employed … in the charging of hand-grenades', but smoke at first obscured him from telling whether the explosion had made a practicable breach. In expectation of a breach at the entrance to the bastion, 'a curtain had been formed with bags of sand, under the shelter of which a picket of forty seamen with their officers had been posted'. Eventually seeing some British soldiers climb into the bastion, he exhorted this picket to oppose them but the Spanish could not be moved; they seemed almost in a state of shock. Velasco rushed up the slope and rallied them but was wounded by a volley from the British, who had quickly formed

**JULY 30
1762**

**El Morro stormed
and captured**

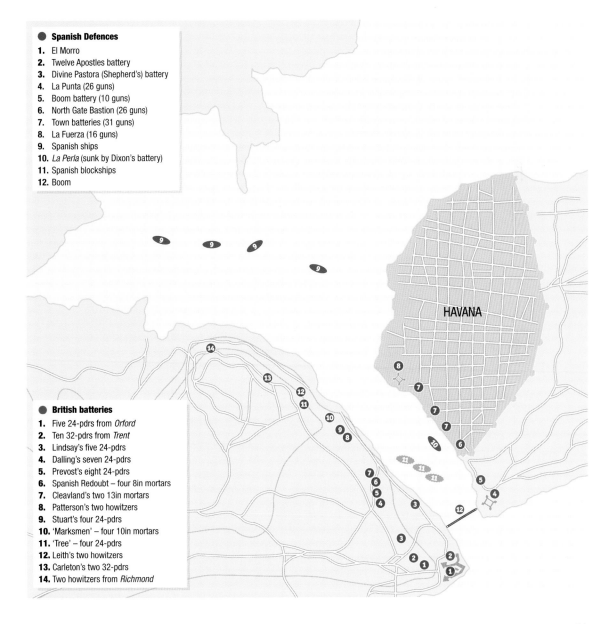

● **Spanish Defences**
1. El Morro
2. Twelve Apostles battery
3. Divine Pastora (Shepherd's) battery
4. La Punta (26 guns)
5. Boom battery (10 guns)
6. North Gate Bastion (26 guns)
7. Town batteries (31 guns)
8. La Fuerza (16 guns)
9. Spanish ships
10. *La Perla* (sunk by Dixon's battery)
11. Spanish blockships
12. Boom

HAVANA

● **British batteries**
1. Five 24-pdrs from *Orford*
2. Ten 32-pdrs from *Trent*
3. Lindsay's five 24-pdrs
4. Dalling's seven 24-pdrs
5. Prevost's eight 24-pdrs
6. Spanish Redoubt – four 8in mortars
7. Cleavland's two 13in mortars
8. Patterson's two howitzers
9. Stuart's four 24-pdrs
10. 'Marksmen' – four 10in mortars
11. 'Tree' – four 24-pdrs
12. Leith's two howitzers
13. Carleton's two 32-pdrs
14. Two howitzers from *Richmond*

Engraved for Mountague's History of England.

The British Troops entering the Breach of the Moro Castle

a firing line. More British troops scrambled across the ditch whilst those first into the bastion moved over the obstruction and around the battlements. Gonzales was killed close to where Velasco was wounded. Montez considered further resistance inside the castle futile, and ordered the garrison to surrender; in the confusion, however, some of the defenders sought refuge in the lighthouse. Here Holyrod was congratulating Nugent on having survived the assault when both men were shot dead. The Spanish then attempted to barricade themselves into the building, but Forbes, furious after seeing his comrades killed, barged open the door and 'put all in it to the sword'.

The fort was 'a heap of ruins'. Besides the two officers, the British had 12 men killed and 28 wounded. The Spanish had 130 dead, 37 wounded, and 326 surrendered (including 16 officers). Of the 213 who tried to escape by crossing the harbour, many were drowned or killed in their boats. Velasco was taken to Havana where he died two days later. In a report to Cleavland, the Secretary to the Admiralty, Pocock described Velasco as 'a brave officer, mortally wounded in defending the colours, sword in hand'. Albemarle suspended hostilities for his funeral.

Capitulation

The Spanish realized the British would build more batteries on La Cabaña to threaten Havana. From the city they fired very briskly, but ineffectively, on El Morro. On 2 August the *Aquilón* was sent down into the harbour entrance and cannonaded the fortress and other positions on La Cabaña, but the following evening departed when fire from British howitzers became too much to bear.

Albemarle knew that if bombardment would not persuade Prado to surrender, storming the city's walls would still be necessary. On 31 July he moved his headquarters to Chorera, and for the first time reconnoitred the ground on that side 'to see in what manner attacks might be carried on with most advantage … in case of occasion'. Mackellar was ordered to Chorera and he identified where approaches to the town could be covered by 'a bank running along shore, from the Lazaro to Fort La Punta, supposing that fort silenced', but advised delay until the batteries on La Cabaña 'had in some measure effected their design; and especially as they might of themselves, perhaps, answer the end without further trouble'.

Mackellar was hoping resistance would collapse after bombardment from La Cabaña. Materials for more batteries were collected 'by the Admiral's assistance'. Prize frigates were broken up to provide wood for gun platforms on which 'thirty carpenters from the Provincial troops, lately arrived, were employed'. However, work still went ahead on entrenchments to the west of the city. On 4 August Park was told to reconnoitre an area for a battery to be built with his section. On his way back he became separated and narrowly avoided 30–40 Spanish soldiers on patrol by taking refuge in a building for the night – an indication that the town's garrison was far from inactive. The Spanish tried to stall the work and 'set some houses near the road on fire, to prevent their being a shelter for us', but on 9 August, 200 men with a covering party of the same number made 'a redoubt on the road to the Punta', even though the Spanish 'began to cannonade along the road pretty warmly'.

On 1 August Ricaud, the chief Spanish engineer, wrote to Prado describing the dangers of the British being able to mount batteries on La Cabaña and the positions being built on the Chorera side. More importantly he told Prado that ammunition was running out and gunners had to limit the number of volleys they fired. The artillery commander, José Crell, confirmed in a report to the war council that there was only enough powder for each bastion to fire five volleys each day for the next six or seven days. Prado ordered nine guns to be placed in hastily made trenches on Manuel Gonzales Hill to defend the shipyard, but after the loss of the grenadiers at El Morro he realized there were not enough regular troops to launch another sortie against the British positions with any prospect of success. A report by Sergeant Major Ramirez showed only 772 regulars fit for duty, including 53 officers; 298 regular soldiers were in hospital.

By 10 August the British batteries on the east side consisted of 'forty-five pieces of cannon, and eight mortars' and were ready to fire. Before the bombardment began, Albemarle sent Prado a summons to capitulate. Prado replied he was 'well assured of carrying on the defence, with strong hopes of a happy exit'. To convince him otherwise, all the British guns opened at daybreak on 11 August. Park described a great firing that day. La Punta and the north bastion of the town were silenced within six hours. At 2.00pm a flag of truce was accepted, and the Spanish asked that 'operations of war be suspended for 24 hours to prepare articles of capitulation that will permit the city to be surrendered'. Prado was now told there was ammunition for only another four or five hours and that only 700 men remained for the city's defence. The next day negotiations continued as the Spanish hoped to retain their shipping, but on 13 August a final threat to recommence the bombardment persuaded them to surrender. The following day Major General Keppel took possession of La Punta, and Howe with his grenadiers occupied the city's land gate. Park wrote the Americans were at last 'at liberty to wash and clean'.

Lieutenant Charles Forbes and the Royal Scots led the assault across the ditch. In identifying Forbes, research has established two probable candidates: the first of the Skellater branch was the son of a Jacobite and brother of General Ian Roy Forbes who died without issue; the second was of the Auchernach branch that would have four sons, all of whom joined the military. The author is thankful to Alex Forbes for this information. (Anne SK Brown collection)

Occupation

Pocock knew the surrender of Havana could not have come sooner. Even though he thought 'the loss of the Spanish fleet will leave all their settlements in this part of the world exposed', he reported his forces were incapable of undertaking further operations. Writing to Egremont, Albemarle described how the army and navy had been reduced to 'a most deplorable and feeble condition' and told Amherst how 'the 17th, Royal Highlanders [42nd], and the 77th are so reduced by sickness that I am obliged to send them to a northern climate in hopes that the change of air may recover them'.

The suffering of the men did not end with the successful conclusion of military operations, and threatened to have serious consequences. On 21 August Albemarle wrote to Egremont that 'unless troops from North America remained there might not be enough manpower available to garrison Havana'. They were retained until October but were suffering just as much. On 16 August Park was taken sick and his illness lasted for six weeks before he died. By 4 September the provincial Lieutenant William Starr commented 'we are now grown so sickly that we do little or nothing'. The Connecticut chaplain, John Graham, described how infected men had a 'dead and dormant look – hands weak, knees feeble, joints trembling – leaning upon staves like men bowed and overloaded with old age'. In Putnam's company, albeit a particularly severe example, 76 died, seven deserted (most before the unit left New York) and only 20 survived.

On 9 October Pocock reported 800 sailors and 500 marines had died, 2,673 seamen and 601 marines were sick and 'we have reason to apprehend several of them will die'. The army's plight was even worse. The example of the 48th Foot was typical: of the 178 men that had managed to reach Havana from New York, 71 died and only 36 enlisted men would return to Ireland in the autumn of 1763. From 7 June to 18 October, 560 officers and men had been killed or died of wounds as a result of the fighting, but 4,708 had succumbed to sickness. Looking after the sick was a huge task. Conditions for the grenadiers and light infantry in a hospital at St Anthony's (in the

On 14 August the *Bonetta* and *Cygnet* sloops helped detach the boom and soldiers were ferried to La Punta and the North Gate. By 21 August the harbour entrance was clear for Pocock to sail in with the fleet. Cash of 1.8 million peso in the treasury was seized, along with goods worth 1 million peso. (Anne SK Brown collection)

middle of town) were so bad, eight carts were pressed into service to move them into the suburbs. By October only 3,000 soldiers were fit for duty.

These losses threatened the ability of the British to occupy Havana. The rest of Cuba was still Spanish and the Governor of Santiago de Cuba had appointed himself the new Captain General of the island; in August he received 600 soldiers from Hispaniola, delivered by Blenac. Only limited measures could be taken to expand British control – Matanzas was occupied by 300 men under the command of Major Moneypenny, and a 50-gun ship was sent to cruise off Cartagena. However, the trading classes were pleased that the trading restrictions were removed. Tobacco and sugar products were exported to Britain to a value of £700,000. Cuban mahogany was also much in demand.

With guerrillas still operating in the interior, military discipline and the maintenance of order were Albemarle's main concerns. He ensured his soldiers did not provoke disturbances. No soldier was to appear in the streets after tattoo and Captain Putnam's duty book tells us 'rum brandy and spirituous liquor [were] prohibited'. To stop soldiers consuming alcohol, patrols were sent out to search those suspected of being involved with its sale.

Mostly locals were free to come and go as they pleased and Albemarle made sure he attended to Spanish complaints. Claims that British officers were quartering themselves on homes not designated for such use led to inspections of these quarters to be made. Soldiers were disciplined, even officers. Captain Francourt of the 56th Foot was actually imprisoned after being accused of stealing a local calash (an open carriage typically with a folding top) and was told he would not be released until he apologized. Officers were told to pay the going rate of one dollar for half a day and only for those carriages labelled for hire.

Morale was helped with the issue of prize money. To ensure the £737,000 collected was distributed to those entitled, each battalion had to provide the paymaster general with a list of all those present on 13 August, the day of the capitulation. The money was divided equally between the army and navy. Each sailor received £3 14s 10d whilst each soldier received £4 1s 8d

Public order was well maintained with few serious incidents to mar the occupation, one exception being the trial of a Spaniard accused of murdering a soldier of the 22nd Foot. Overall Pocock could report 'all things appear very quiet and easy'. (National Maritime Museum)

THE INVESTMENT AND SURRENDER OF HAVANA

11 JUNE–12 AUGUST 1762

Albemarle's army quickly finds itself under pressure. With seven battalions posted at Guanabacoa and no sign of the troops from New York, the soldiers constructing the batteries in front of El Moro are committed to excessive labour with no guaranteed water supply and the impending threat of tropical disease hanging over them. The fate of the expedition is in doubt.

▼ EVENTS ON THE COJIMAR SIDE

A Spanish Redoubt and mortar batteries built to target Spanish shipping 13–24 June.

B Elliot evacuates Guanabacoa and pulls back to siege camp on 15 July.

C Batteries built on the Cabanas after the fall of El Moro, 2–10 August and open on 11 August.

D La Punta and North Bastion silenced within six hours.

KEY

Movements of 11 June

Movements of 15 June–14 July

Movements of 15 July–14 August

▼ EVENTS ON THE CHORERA SIDE

1 Chorera castle captured on 11 June.

2 Howe lands to guarantee water supply on 15 June and pushes inland.

3 Redoubt built on San Antonio Hill.

4 Batteries to interdict harbour channel open on 16 July, Spanish sally on 18 July spikes them temporarily.

5 Canal diverted from Havana into marsh.

6 Howe takes Luz Hill near Jesu del Monte on 1 August.

7 Prado establishes battery on Gonzales Hill on 1 August.

8 Provincials from New York push forward along road to La Punta in early August.

(in comparison a lieutenant received £80), which could be spent on the pleasures of the city by those that remained healthy. Both Pocock and Albemarle received a third of their service's share – £123,000. A notice that 'gentlemen performers are requested to meet the managers tomorrow at Loids coffee house' showed that more refined entertainment was also available.

Redeployment

After the capitulation the fleet soon started to disperse. On 16 August the *Cambridge* escorted a convoy from Jamaica to Britain. On 19 August the *Centaur* and *Defiance* departed for Halifax after news came of a French landing at St John's. On 30 August the *Sutherland* and *Dover*, with their lower deck guns removed to accommodate Prado, Hevia, the Viceroy of Peru, and Governor of Cartagena, departed Havana accompanied by transports carrying 1,000 Spanish soldiers and 1,200 sailors to be repatriated. (Once Prado was home a triumvirate of ministers sentenced him to death; the king commuted the sentence to ten years' imprisonment but he died in confinement in 1770.) On 6 September Blenac sailed for France with five ships of the line and two frigates, and on 12 October Keppel, appointed Rear Admiral, sailed to Jamaica with seven ships of the line: *Valiant, Orford, Temeraire, Edgar, Alcide, Nottingham,* and *Pembroke,* and the two frigates *Trent* and *Richmond.*

Before Pocock left Havana, the *Stirling Castle* was found to be leaking and was sunk in the harbour, the ship's crew moving to the *Infante* with Elphinston appointed as captain. Pocock eventually departed for home in early November and was beset by the very storms he feared in the Caribbean. He sailed with the *Namur, Culloden, Marlborough, Devonshire, Temple,* 49 transports, one ordnance ship, three bomb ketches, and the *San Jenero, Infante* and *Assumption* prizes (leaving *Belle-Isle, Rippon, Hampton Court,* eight transports, three hospital ships, and two ordnance ships at Havana). After passing the Florida Keys, a gale separated the *Marlborough* from the rest of the fleet and as it was taking on water, the crew were taken off by a passing convoy heading for Newfoundland. Another violent storm wrought great destruction 600 miles from the Isles of Scilly; the *Temple, Devonshire* and 12 transports were lost – the time spent in the tropics had done nothing for their seaworthiness. Closer to home, the *San Jenero* prize was wrecked passing the Downs.

On 24 October the Americans went home escorted by *Intrepid,* carrying 680 Connecticut men, 343 New Yorkers, 149 from New Jersey and 119 Rhode Islanders, but many were suffering and a quarter died on the journey. According to Putnam, so many regulars tried to abscond with them that a pardon was offered 'to the regiment they properly belong'. Many of the colonial veterans would serve under Washington. (Captain Gates, Monckton's ADC in 1762, commanded the Continentals at Saratoga in 1777.)

Many soldiers were discharged and took advantage of free land grants in America: 50 acres for a private and 5,000 for an officer. These men would later predominantly fight for the loyalist cause during the American War of Independence. There were exceptions, like Major Montgomery of the 17th

Foot who settled in America and became a brigadier in the Continental Army before being killed in 1776 trying to capture Quebec. Others returned to Britain and served in static garrisons; some, if their wounds were severe and their service had been long – and this applied to provincials as well – could be approved for a place in, or at least receive a pension (a paltry 5d per day) from, Chelsea.

Few regular soldiers that remained in their units managed to return home quickly. Of the 41 battalions in the Americas in 1762, as many as 23 were still there in 1764 (a year after the war's end). Miller described how transports carrying his unit (the 15th Foot) back to Britain were stopped before leaving the Gulf of Florida, and told to proceed to Canada. He came home only in 1768 having spent ten years away. Forcing the colonists to contribute to the costs of maintaining these units in America would lead to resentment that, supported by the French and Spanish who were now implacable enemies of Britain, would ultimately turn into an unstoppable rebellion.

Peace

In his official dispatch, Pocock wrote how he hoped the capture of Havana 'may prove the saving of lives in the future ... by obtaining a safe and honourable peace'. The achievement was celebrated that year in the Annual Register as 'the most decisive conquest we have had since the beginning of the war'. In America, especially the Carolinas and Georgia where the threat of Spanish raiding parties was keenly felt, the news generated raucous celebration with bonfires and self-congratulatory sermons. However, seizure of the most valuable Spanish possession in the Caribbean surprised many in Whitehall, and threatened to upset finely balanced negotiations for a general peace. Bute, who believed in a balance of power, said to a colleague how the taking of the city 'has turned the heads of the wisest men and those most inclined to peace'. The talk in the coffee houses in London and the comment in the papers was of the scandalous distribution of prize money and the ravages of disease; war-weariness had set in. Sympathy for returning soldiers could be conditional though. At the opera, Boswell commented that when two Highland officers recently returned from Havana came in there were cries for them to be removed.

Spain found it impossible to prosecute the war any longer and agreed to hand over all its possessions east of the Mississippi (including Florida) to guarantee Havana's return. Many in Britain regarded this as poor compensation. Surprisingly, Spain actually gained new territory in America; because France had returned Minorca to Britain rather than to Spain, France bought Spanish compliance with the peace agreement by giving over all French lands in Louisiana west of the Mississippi in recompense. On 10 February 1763 the Peace of Paris, which agreed these provisions, was signed. Five months later, on 6 July 1763, the last British troops left Havana.

ANALYSIS

In early 1762 Britain took prompt action to deal with a potentially devastating new enemy. Pitt had warned about the Spanish danger since the previous autumn and, although his downfall brought a more pacific cabinet into power, intelligence reports continued to betray Spanish intentions of joining the coalition at war with Britain. The country had to be defeated before becoming troublesome. The expedition to capture Havana, the epicentre of Spanish trade in the New World, was therefore conceived to force Spain out of the war. Spain considered Havana impregnable and Britain sought to exploit perceived Spanish complacency about its defence. Because forces were already mobilized, various elements of the expedition could be gathered quickly. A small expeditionary force was dispatched to join a squadron of ships and 8,000 soldiers already in the Caribbean involved in the capture of Martinique. Also, as the French had been thrown out of Canada, reinforcements could come down from New York. Despite the sheer scale of these preparations, the Spanish failed to discover the destination of the expedition.

The expedition was not without risk. If the French and Spanish navies had co-operated, then British command of the sea – an essential prerequisite for an amphibious operation on this scale – could have been threatened. In the Caribbean, Rodney had sent Douglas to Jamaica and

Prado was criticized for not burning the fleet and the following, shown in this picture by Serres, were seized: *Aquilón* (*74*), *Conquistador* (74), *Reina* (70), *San Antonio* (64), *Tigre* (70), *San Jenero* (60), *África* (70), *America* (60), *Infante* (74), and *Soberano* (74). *San Carlos* (80) and *Santiago* (60 or 80) were also taken on the stocks. (National Maritime Museum)

when Pocock arrived, was unable to provide him with sufficient escorts. Instead of waiting for Rodney's ships to return to Martinique, Pocock quickly assessed the immediate threat to Jamaica as negligible, and arranged for a rendezvous with Douglas closer to the Old Bahama Channel. He was, however, aided by Douglas who, using his own initiative, sent Captain Hervey to watch the French squadron at Cape François and Captain Elphinston (in the *Richmond*) to chart the channel. As a result, Pocock was able to navigate a potentially treacherous passage free from enemy interference. The approach through the channel was daring and designed to maintain secrecy. The losses suffered by both American convoys showed what could have befallen Pocock. The British arrived at Havana to find the Spanish fleet still in port and before any last-minute defensive preparations could be properly set in hand.

Commanders had to cope with a unique combination of conditions in the Caribbean. Uppermost in the navy's mind was the importance of gaining a secure anchorage to protect against a hurricane. In 1741 at Cartagena, Admiral Vernon's overriding concern had been to break into the harbour; at Havana, Pocock utilized nearby bays at Chorera and Mariel. The paramount concern of the army was tropical disease, which would start affecting the men within six weeks. Albemarle needed to construct enough batteries to silence the enemy's cannon and be capable of breaching the town's walls in order to carry out, or at least threaten, a successful assault before disease debilitated the strength of his troops. At Havana, the labour required to build these siege works on rocky, sloping ground in a hot and humid climate was substantial. Initially he was comparatively well off for manpower; however, a substantial proportion had to be employed foraging, guarding, and collecting water. Then there were the delays through enemy action or tactical mistakes.

The benefits of a quick and orderly landing in flat-bottomed boats could be useful if exploited correctly. The rapid landing in these boats limited the time available for Prado to attend to defects in his defences, which he had

**AUGUST 13
1762**

**Havana
surrenders**

known about but had not remedied. Albemarle's march inland nearly wasted this advantage. If it was not for Howe's probes up on La Cabaña and Spanish perceptions of the insecurity of their hastily constructed positions there, the Spanish defence of La Cabaña may have been more resolute, in which case the siege of El Morro could have been significantly delayed. As it was, La Cabaña heights, in a position to dominate both El Morro and some of the harbour, were soon stormed. Construction of a battery in front of El Morro could then be safely begun. However, to contend as David Syrett did that flat-bottomed boats 'enabled the British to exploit the strategic advantages gained from naval superiority' is perhaps to forget that the amphibious operations also included drawn-out siege operations.

Albemarle and Keppel competently conducted the siege, except for the initial siting of the Grand Battery. El Morro, with its ditch in front, was never going to fall quickly, as Spanish reinforcements and *matériel* could be ferried across the harbour from the town. This helped the defenders to remount their guns during the night and enabled two Spanish counterattacks on 29 June and 21 July, each with around 1,000 men, which came close to severely delaying the siege works. The ditch also significantly delayed the taking of the fort and threatened to ruin the whole enterprise, but the very feature that concealed it from Knowles – the knife-edge of rock keeping out the sea – permitted the miners to access the foot of the bastion and dig shafts for explosives. Laying the mines in such circumstances were courageous acts that could not be taken for granted.

Albemarle has been criticized for concentrating on El Morro rather than the town. The historian Tom Pocock described him as leisurely and conventional as he 'avoided the most practical course, an attack on the weakly defended walls of the city itself, in favour of the conventional setting up and opening of siege batteries'. However, this view seems to give little weight to the assessment of Havana's defences made by the chief engineer, Mackellar. He realized that once the fortress was captured the British would be free to build more batteries on La Cabaña to bombard Havana. He also appreciated that an approach against the town's walls on the other side of the harbour would be vulnerable to attacks from the very large garrison, known to be around 8,000 men, as well as fire from El Morro. Both Albemarle and Pocock accepted their expert's analysis. A pre-emptive assault against strong defences would probably have been a disaster. Prado capitulated because he knew he could not repel the attackers; after being besieged for six weeks his garrison was exhausted and ammunition was low.

The conduct of the operation received contemporary criticism from Rear Admiral Knowles, who perhaps rightly regarded the early march inland as a diversion from the primary objective of La Cabaña. He also asserted with some justification that the Grand Battery, sited too close to El Morro, could have been overwhelmed soon after opening; it was only because the navy distracted El Morro's fire onto their ships that it survived longer. However, when stating that the siege could have been completed in half the time, he appears to show little appreciation of the full rigours of constructing siege works in the tropics. This was not the first time he was critical of the army;

having been at the siege of Cartagena in 1741, he wrote a book in which he blamed General Wentworth for that failed operation.

Turning to the role of the navy at Havana, their main function was to safely transport the army to the points of debarkation, and then act as a deterrent to any naval attack either from within or without the harbour. The naval bombardment of El Morro failed to dismantle El Morro's defences, but did divert Spanish attention from the land batteries. Ships of the line were very powerful instruments of war, each broadside having more weight of shot than a land battery. This was very effective against forts close to the beaches but less useful against those farther away or on high cliffs, such as El Morro. Without doubt the navy's most important contribution was the support it provided to the army once landed. In 1741 at Cartagena, the unwillingness of the naval commanders to commit to the expedition had contributed significantly to the army's defeat. In 1762 the co-operation of the navy in providing manpower and supplies was vital for the army to function.

The idea that amphibious warfare in the 18th century was part of a new military capability that enhanced the strategic effect of the Royal Navy in the tropics ignores the improvements in colonial fortifications, which meant amphibious forces more often than not experienced the drudgery and attrition of siege warfare. Fortifications in the Caribbean, far from being of 'doubtful value' as the historian Pares contended, guaranteed colonial possessions and much effort and many lives had to be expended to capture them. Large forces were required and as these could not be maintained locally, they had to be transported from Europe or North America. The dangers of transferring thousands of men and tons of equipment across the oceans and deploying them against Caribbean defences in the necessary size to achieve success were significant, and could lead to terrible disaster.

Successful amphibious landings were often the result of surprise and this was easier to achieve with smaller forces, which in part explains why spectacular assaults from the sea were more commonplace in the 16th and 17th centuries. In the 18th century, and at Havana in particular, a positive outcome was by no means guaranteed. The men worked in terrible conditions and suffered horribly. However, uniquely for an amphibious operation in the Caribbean, Albemarle had a large army of over 15,000 men available and, crucially, the support of naval personnel. In addition, the timely arrival of the convoys from New York enabled him to protect the siege works near Chorera and gave him confidence in his ability to maintain his conquest after the capitulation of the town. The capture of Havana was not an achievement that would be easily matched in the years to come.

For amphibious operations on the coast of France, manpower was more readily available and the absence of tropical disease meant expeditions were not subject to the same time constraints. However, even here there were difficulties. Bad weather was a constant hazard and relieving enemy forces were much more likely to appear. In addition, a scarcity of suitable beaches meant landings were often carried out far from the objective, and as defending forces could live off the land more easily, they could operate against the invader's supply lines.

CONCLUSION

The expedition to capture Havana was one of the most ambitious amphibious operations conducted in the 18th century. Daringly conceived and competently executed, the city was secured for the British and was a weighty bargaining chip in the peace negotiations the following year. British expeditionary warfare had come of age. Spanish involvement in the Seven Years War was ended by a single operation, an effect the government tried to replicate against the Turks at Gallipoli some 150 years later. More immediately, during the Napoleonic Wars, Britain was able to deliver land forces to the extremities of Napoleon's Empire to help foment revolt against his rule.

A coin was struck to commemorate the defence of El Morro, showing Velasco and Gonzales on one side and the mine exploding on this the reverse side. Charles III gave Velasco's widow a pension and his brother a peerage. The Spanish Navy has always maintained a serving ship named after Velasco. (National Maritime Museum)

The expeditious assembly of the units in England, the co-ordination in bringing disparate forces together in the Caribbean, and the secrecy with which this was done caught the Spanish unawares. Albemarle has been accused of being too cautious, not taking advantage of a successful landing by quickly storming the walls. This is too severe; the strength of the fortifications and determination of the defenders meant a methodical approach was required, but as with most military operations this did not guarantee success. Fortunately, the opportune arrival of the troops from New York compensated for setbacks in the siege works that could have led to the expedition failing through disease.

The effects of disease on the besiegers, who conducted heavy toil in horrendous conditions, meant manpower was at a premium. At Cartagena in 1741, the failure of the services to work together led to disastrous results and no reward. In 1762 co-operation of army and navy commanders secured logistical links between the forces ashore and those at sea. The navy provided sailors to help move stores, formed marines into two battalions of troops to operate ashore, and maintained their own batteries against El Morro to decisive effect.

Yet the deployment of British forces to the Caribbean, even though successful, was a double-edged sword. The losses suffered at Havana meant the Crown's defences on the North American

continent became severely weakened. In 1764 an Indian rebellion spread from Lake Superior to the Mississippi Delta. The survivors from Havana were needed but were in no fit state, and of 12 forts attacked only four held out. The British became more conscious of the Indian threat than ever before, but the annual cost of an effective defence would be £500,000. Much to the chagrin of the colonies, the military budget had to be increased because too many men had been consumed by the Havana operation. Paradoxically, by trying to take advantage of command of the sea, the future security of Britain's American colonies, which was ultimately guaranteed by those who fought on land, was put in jeopardy.

The bombardment by the batteries on La Cabaña targeted the Spanish batteries in the town. There was no effective response due to lack of ammunition and the North Bastion and La Punta were quickly overwhelmed. (Anne SK Brown collection)

BIBLIOGRAPHY

Anderson, Fred, *Crucible of War*, London (2000)

Anon., *An Authentic Journal of the Siege of Havana by an Officer*, London (1762)

Beatson, Robert, *Naval and Military Memoirs of Great Britain from 1727 to 1783*, 6 vols., London (1804)

Brooks, Richard, *The Royal Marines: The History of the Royal Marines 1664–2000*, London (2002)

Brumwell, Stephen, *Redcoats: The British Soldier and War in the Americas 1755–1763*, Cambridge (2002)

Burton, Robert, 'The Siege and Capture of Havana in 1762' in *Maryland Historical Magazine*, Vol.4 pp.321–35 (1909)

Campbell, Bruce, *Redcoats and Yellow Fever*, Providence, Rhode Island (1991)

Chartrand, René, *The Spanish Main 1492–1800*, Oxford (2006)

Chawner, W. Hampden, 'The Capture of Havana' in *United Service Magazine*, Vol.40, pp.87–91 (1904)

Corbett, J. S., *England in the Seven Years' War: A Study in Combined Strategy*, London (1907)

Gardiner, Asa Bird, 'Havana Expedition of 1762 in the War with Spain', Rhode Island Historical Society (1898)

Harbron, John, *Trafalgar and the Spanish Navy*, London (1988)

Harding, Richard, *Amphibious Warfare in the Eighteenth Century*, Rochester (1991)

Hart, Francis Russell, *The Siege of Havana, 1762*, Boston (1932)

Keppel, Sonia, *Three Brothers at Havana, 1762*, Guildford (1981)

Mackellar, Patrick, *A correct journal of the landing His Majesty's forces on the island of Cuba and of the siege and surrender of the Havannah, August 13, 1762*, London (1762)

Mante, Thomas, *A History of the Late War in North America and the Islands of the West Indies*, London (1772)

McLynn, Frank, *1759: The Year of Victories*, London (2004)

McNeill, J. R., *Atlantic Empires of France and Spain: Havana and Louisbourg 1700–63*, North Carolina (1984)

Middleton, Richard, *The Bells of Victory*, Cambridge (1985)

Pares, Richard, *War and Trade in the West Indies, 1739–62*, Oxford (1936)

Park, Roswell, *A Journal of the Expedition Against Cuba*, Buffalo (1920)

Placer Cervero, Gustavo, *Los Defensores del Morro*, Havana (2003)

Pocock, Tom, *Battle for Empire*, London (1998)

Putnam, Israel, *The Two Putnams, Israel and Rufus: In the Havana Expedition, 1762, and in the Mississippi River Expedition, 1772–73*, Hartford Connecticut (1931)

Robertson, Archibald, *His Diaries and Sketches in North America 1762–80*, New York (1971)

Rodger, N. A. M., *Command of the Ocean: A Naval History of Britain 1649–1815*, London (2004)

Rogers, Col. H. C. B., *Troopships and Their History*, London (1963)

Russett, Alan, *Dominic Serres, R. A., 1719–1793: War Artist to the Navy*, Woodbridge (2001)

Sanchez-Galarraga, Jorge, 'Luis de Velasco at the Siege of Havana, 1762' in *Seven Years War Association Journal*, Vol.XII, No.2

Schumm, Matt, & Schweizer, Karl, *The Seven Years War: A Transatlantic History*, London (2008)

Smelser, Marshall, *The Campaign for the Sugar Islands 1759: A study of amphibious warfare*, Virginia (1955)

Syrett, David, 'American Provincials and the Havana Campaign of 1762' in *New York History*, Vol.49, pp.375–90 (1968)

Syrett, David, 'The British Landing at Havana: An Example of an Eighteenth Century Combined Operation' in *Mariners Mirror*, Vol.55, pp.325–31 (1969)

Syrett, David, 'The Methodology of British Amphibious Operations during the Seven Years' and American Wars', *Mariners Mirror*, vol.59, pp.269–80 (1972)

Syrett, David, *The Siege and Capture of Havana, 1762*, London (1970)

INDEX